THE
AGILE
ADMINISTRATOR

George R. Allen

Doctor of Business Administration
THE AMERICAN UNIVERSITY,
Washington, D.C.

Tempe Publishers
Tempe, Arizona

ACKNOWLEDGEMENTS: My Special Thanks

to Douglas C. Schaefer of Waterloo, Ontario, Canada, who created the original drawings used throughout the book.

to those administrators and faculty members and other persons who gave me the ideas and material, intentionally and otherwise.

to Dr. Kelly Black for encouraging me to publish the manuscript.

to Joanne, Karen, Richard, and Barbara—all 'agiles' in their own way.

to Mary Ognjanov for making a book out of a rough manuscript.

Copyright © 1979, by George R. Allen

Requests for permission to reproduce any portion of the book (or for copies of the book) should be sent to: TEMPE PUBLISHERS, P.O. Box 1321, Tempe, Arizona, 85281.

First Printing, 1979

Manufactured in the United States of America by TEMPE PUBLISHERS

Library of Congress Catalog Card Number: 79-65136

ISBN: 0-933554-12-5

Printed in the United States of America by IMPERIAL LITHO/GRAPHICS, Phoenix, AZ.

Preface

Has anyone evaluated your job performance? Have you evaluated others? Do you work for anyone? Does anyone work for you? If you answer "YES" to any of these questions then you should enjoy this *satire on the personnel evaluation process.*

The purpose of satire is to entertain and to (hopefully) reform. These are the twin objectives of this book. I have tried to present material that is soundly based in fact, avoids exaggeration, and blends together the proper proportions of humor and criticism—essential ingredients of satire.

Three concepts form the basis for this look at the machinations behind the distribution of rewards in organizations of all kinds:

THE BASIC SUPPOSITION (THE B.S.) If an administrator LIKES a person being evaluated, then recommendations regarding that person will *tend* to be POSITIVE in nature. If an administrator DISLIKES a person being evaluated, then recommendations regarding that person will *tend* to be NEGATIVE in nature.

THE LAW OF INVERSE EVALUATION (THE L.I.E.) For every piece of data regarding a person's performance and qualifications, there are two EQUAL BUT OPPOSITE INTERPRETATIONS, both plausible and apparently based upon sound logic.

THE AGILE ADMINISTRATOR (THE A.A.) An Agile Administrator is a person who is able to interpret all available data regarding performance and qualifications in such a manner that the interpretation will support either a POSITIVE or NEGATIVE recommendation. He or she operates under THE BASIC SUPPOSITION and uses THE LAW OF INVERSE EVALUATION in all recommendations.

A generous supply of quotes appear throughout the book. They are included to provide a wealth of wisdom in a few words, and to add wit (I hope) to my words! An effort was made to identify the source of each quote. When no one could be credited, the quote was ascribed to the most quoted couple in literature, Mr. and Mrs. Anonymous.

These quotes contain the distilled wisdom of some of the greatest minds of the past and present. I urge you to read each one twice.

I urge you to read each one twice! Each quote has a solid message to send if you are receptive.

This satire on the personnel evaluation process will be interpreted by some readers as truthful, humorous, accurate, satirical, and in other *positive* ways. It will be interpreted by others as untrue, inaccurate, cynical, sarcastic, and in other *negative* ways. There is no way for me to prevent such polar interpretations. In fact, such divergent opinions merely demonstrate THE LAW OF INVERSE EVALUATION (THE L.I.E.) in action.

This book is needed and I am glad that I had the chance to write it. Should it also prove to be a modest financial success, the publisher should be happy too,—since he is me.

George R. Allen
Tempe, Arizona
June, 1979

WHAT IS SATIRE?

"Satire is the art of stepping on somebody's toes so that he feels it but doesn't holler." – Helmut Qualtinger.

"Satire is to take the utmost trouble to find the right thing to say, and to say it with the utmost levity." – Adapted from George Bernard Shaw.

"Satire is to study the abnormal as the best way to understand the normal." – Adapted from William James.

"Satire asks each person to reform himself, in order to contribute his full share towards the reformation of his neighbors." – Adapted from Norman Douglas.

"Satire is a sort of glass wherein beholders do generally discover everybody's face but their own." – Jonathan Swift.

Table of Contents

List of Exhibits

An Agile Administrator. . . .

. . . avoids the small errors as he sweeps on to the grand fallacy. – Adapted from Benjamin Stolberg.

. . . stands with both feet firmly planted in mid-air, on both sides of an issue. – Adapted from Homer Ferguson.

. . . makes his conscience not his guide, but his accomplice. – Adapted from Benjamin Disraeli.

. . . does not stand on his own record but jumps on the other fellow's. – Anon.

. . . realizes that you can't fool all of the people all of the time, but is satisfied with a majority. – Anon.

. . . will not believe what he sees, because he is too busy speculating about what he does not see. – Adapted from La Bovier de Fontenello.

. . . will always claim that he has a right to argue about issues which he does not understand. – Adapted from several sources.

. . . is forever poised between a cliche and an indiscretion. – Adapted from Harold MacMillan.

. . . has the facility to exaggerate the importance of some pieces of data, and to completely overlook the deficiency of others. – Adapted from Hugh Stevenson Tigner.

. . . is a person who takes ideas and facts which we understand, and makes them sound confusing. – Anon.

1 Foundations for Performance Evaluation

"Man is a reasoning rather than a reasonable animal."
                                        – Robert B. Hamilton.

"Politeness is one half good nature, and the other half good lying."   – Mary Wilson Little.

"When everybody is somebody then nobody is anybody."
                                        – Anon.

"Practical politics means ignoring facts."
                                        – Henry Brooks Adams.

1.0   FOUNDATIONS FOR PERFORMANCE EVALUATION

"The performance evaluation process is a perpetual caricature of itself; and every moment it is the mockery and the contradiction of what it is pretending to be." – Adapted from George Santayana.

Millions of people each year are subjected to an evaluation of their performance and qualifications to determine how they will participate in the reward systems of their organizations. This book is about that evaluation process. In these trying days of affirmative action programs, claims of discrimination, and the tendency to consult one's lawyer at the slightest hint of getting a negative rating or evaluation, the personnel evaluation process requires skillful handling. Fortunately (or unfortunately, depending upon your point of view), managers, supervisors, and administrators have risen to the occasion and are blithely weaving their way through the evaluation process— often to the consternation and detriment of those being evaluated.

Administrators who are performing these annual evaluations have become extremely adept at the process, so much so that I have classified them as *Agile Administrators.*[1] The full impact of this term is not widely understood, but is becoming more apparent each day. This book is an attempt to reveal the high level of sophistication achieved by Agile Administrators, and to present a satirical (yet serious) look at the performance evaluation process.

In order to achieve my objective, three concepts have been formulated:

1. The Law of Inverse Evaluation (The L.I.E.)
2. The Basic Supposition (The B.S.)
3. The Agile Administrator (The A.A.)

These concepts are described in this chapter, which lays the foundation for the evaluation process. First, let's look at the Law of Inverse Evaluation!

---

[1]The term "Administrator" will be used to refer to any person who has complete or partial responsibility for evaluating the performance and credentials of others in order to make decisions on hiring, firing, promoting, salaries, etc.

1.1 THE LAW OF INVERSE EVALUATION (The L.I.E.)

"Get your facts first, then you can distort them as much as you please." – Mark Twain.

Two or more persons witnessing an event or hearing about some statement of fact may reach *opposite interpretations* about the same piece of information. In the *sporting world* these polar interpretations are relatively obvious. When a batter hits a home run (baseball), a touchdown is scored (football), a basket is scored (basketball), a goal is made (hockey), etc., the event is interpreted as the *best* thing that can happen for the team making the score and the *worst* thing that can happen to the opponent. Fans will interpret the event in opposite fashion, depending upon whether it happens *for* or *against* their team. In all such cases, *the event is the same,* but the interpretations of the event are completely opposite.

In *politics* the Law of Inverse Evaluation is slightly less obvious, but still there. A YOUNG politician will view his youth as an *asset,* implying a fresh viewpoint and no responsibility for the current political situation (which could be better no matter how good it is). His OLDER opponent sees youth as a *liability,* implying inexperience, lack of political astuteness, etc. Conversely, the old politician views his age as an asset, implying wisdom, experience, and the knowledge of having been involved in politics for a given length of time. His younger opponent views his "aged opponent" as responsible for the current situation, out of touch with the present, antiquated in his thinking, etc. Thus, age is seen as an asset when you are old and as a liability when you are young. Youth is interpreted in a positive manner when one is young, and in a negative manner when one is older.

Further, if a *political leader* takes some firm action, he is touted by his supporters as providing the kind of leadership that is needed and dictated by the office held. His political opponents, on the other hand, accuse him of being a tyrant, an autocrat, or a dictator, or of otherwise interfering with the free enterprise system. But if that same person refrains from taking an action, his political opponents accuse him of failing to carry out the functions of his office, or of failing to provide the needed leadership, etc. His supporters, however, view the inaction as giving the democratic processes an opportunity to operate.

Completely contradictory interpretations are even in evidence in the *medical* field. A jogger gets concerned when his pulse rate rises (during exercise) to 170 beats per minute. One doctor tells him that this is *a good sign,* since a diseased heart could not rise to this high level. Another doctor tells him that it is *a bad sign,* because if he were in condition the heart would not have to work as hard during exercise. Here we have the same pulse rate, but very contrasting interpretations.

In the *academic world,* there are innumerable examples of the Law of Inverse Evaluation. When a professor is objective in grading, students think that the material or course is too subjective to be viewed in such an objective manner. Should the professor take a subjective approach, then students feel that the material and course are too objective for a subjective approach. If the professor *assigns* members to a group, then students feel that they should be allowed to *select* which group they join for group projects. Should the professor let them select their own groups, then students feel that he has shifted the burden to them. When assignments are given in a text and discussed in class, then students complain that they already know what they have read, and think that the professor should elaborate on the material and not just cover it. Should he fail to cover the material, then the complaint is that they should not be asked to read the material if it is not going to be covered in class.

Why data and events can be viewed in such polar fashion can be explained by The General L.I.E. Statement. *For every fact there are equal and opposite interpretations, depending upon the BIASED point of view of those who perceive the fact.* In the personnel evaluation process—the subject of this book—this statement is narrowed to form the L.I.E.

EXHIBIT 1.
THE LAW OF INVERSE EVALUATION (The L.I.E.)

The Law of Inverse Evaluation states that for every piece of data regarding performance and qualifications, there are two equal but opposite interpretations, both plausible and apparently based upon sound logic.[2]

---

[2]This may sound like a paraphrasing of Newton's Law of Physics, that "for every action there is an equal and opposite reaction." It is! This permits me to footnote Newton, a scholar of some repute, thus making this book more scholarly. There is an implied and direct positive relationship between the number of footnotes and the scholarly rating of a publication.

Whether information regarding one's performance or qualifications is good or bad, favorable or unfavorable, desirable or undesirable, beneficial or detrimental, is only in a small way connected to the information itself. The interpretation is largely a function of the person who is reviewing and evaluating the information. When one is being evaluated for hiring, promotion, or salary increases, or simply to decide if a person is to be retained or terminated, the information which is used to base the decision upon is only as important and relevant as the evaluator wishes it to be.

When completely opposite interpretations can be reached from any data being analyzed, it is little wonder that there are inadvertent misinterpretations and interpretations which are highly suspect. Is there, in fact, only one correct way to interpret data on performance and qualifications? Is it legitimate to accept that interpretation which fits into a preconceived and preordained viewpoint, that is, one which reflects our personal likes and dislikes? Yet, that is exactly what happens all too often. But it is done with such aplomb and grace that the evaluator cannot be caught in a lie, and cannot be accused of anything that is illegal. Is it his fault that equal and opposite interpretations are plausible, and that he has chosen one that is opposite to yours (or that you have chosen one that is opposite to his)?

Honest disagreements on matters of fact can exist. Honest interpretations can be made which may eventually prove to have been incorrect, despite the initial intentions of the evaluator. But the eagerness of some administrators to concoct interpretations of data which are spurious at best is just another clear signal that the Law of Inverse Evaluation is at work, and what I will later call the Basic Supposition underlies such seemingly contradictory interpretations.

Now the initials L.I.E. may seem to imply that I am accusing administrators of lying when they justify personnel recommendations with unique and personally biased interpretations of data. This is not my point or purpose at all! In fact, few of the administrators I know are out-and-out liars—only those who do not understand the nuances of the Law of Inverse Evaluation! There is no need for administrators to resort to lies.[3] It will become increasingly obvious that an administrator is perfectly capable of supporting any recommendation he wishes to make on the basis of any data that is presented to him for evaluation.

---

[3]Although lies are often justified as expedient exaggerations! "What is intended as a little white lie often ends as a double feature in technicolor." Madena R. Wallingford.

Herzog makes a good case that, indeed, "The Lie is Dead." He reasons that:

> "For the liar (who is, after all, the perpetrator of lies) the outright lie has always presented an enormous and central peril—that of being exposed, with the humiliation and even jail sentence which may follow. So clumsy and even hazardous a weapon cried out to be replaced by something that would accomplish the lie's objectives and be at the same time safe."[4]

Herzog concluded that the B.S. Factor replaced the lie.

> "The B.S. Factor . . . causes a subtle skewing of sense, a distortion of meaning, without ever becoming a lie. Conventional lies wear thin sooner or later, but the Fake Factor is immensely durable, being a dense weave of logical errors and sophistries known since antiquity, combined or recycled into spectacular new combinations with current prejudices and inanities, defenses of failure and denials of guilt, and the modern religion of science. . . the consequence, overall, is cant and obfuscation of such an extent that a cerebral fog has settled upon our mental landscape, all but obliterating its real features."[5]

It is my contention that the Law of Inverse Evaluation replaced the lie in the personnel evaluation process, and is at work wherever employee performance and qualifications are evaluated.

The liar lacks a degree of sophistication in the use of the L.I.E. Liars are unable to think intelligently enough to avoid the need for lying, but can continue to lie because they are protected from exposure.

> "Proof of lies and outright falsehoods is time-consuming, costly, and not without significant risks. To expose an administrator is to expose oneself to recriminations, real or imagined. This fear of reprisals has been an adequate weapon to maintain the system so far . . ."[6]

---

[4]For this quote, and more information, see *The B.S. Factor,* Arthur Herzog, Simon and Schuster, New York, New York, 1973, Chapter 1, "The Death of Lies."
[5]Ibid, *The B.S. Factor.*
[6]Ibid., *The B.s. Factor.*

Many exaggerations, distortions and manipulations of data are completely within the bounds of moral, ethical, and legal propriety, but nonetheless are highly suspect.[7] (*"There are three kinds of lies: lies, damned lies, and statistics."* – Benjamin Disraeli.)

The truth can be stated in such a fashion or presented in such a manner that the real meaning is lost, and only one logical conclusion emerges—one which is devoid of reality and contrary to fact. (*"Truth does not consist of minute accuracy of detail, but in conveying the right impression."* – Lord Alford.)

To see why exaggerations and distortions occur, let's discuss what appears to be largely responsible: the Basic Supposition.

1.2   THE BASIC SUPPOSITION (The B.S.)

"Attitudes are more important than facts." – Norman Vincent Peale.

Many people have the mistaken impression that data on performance and qualifications is *input* to the evaluation process, and the *output* of the evaluation is a recommendation that is either positive or negative. Such is not always the case. The reverse is often true. The Agile Administrator knows what recommendation he is going to make, and merely consults the data on performance and qualifications to *develop the rationale* to support the action. This predisposition to act, this pre-judging of individuals, is a manifestation of the Basic Supposition!

EXHIBIT 2.
THE BASIC SUPPOSITION (The B.S.)

   A. If an administrator *likes* a person being evaluated, then recommendations regarding that person will *tend to be positive* in nature.
   B. If an administrator *dislikes* a person being evaluated, then recommendations regarding that person will *tend to be negative* in nature.

Notice that the Basic Supposition does not state that an administrator will make positive recommendations about those people he

---

[7]For complete details, see *How to Lie with Statistics,* Darrell Huff, W. W. Norton and Company, Inc., New York, New York, 1954.

likes, or that he will make negative recommendations about those he dislikes. It merely states that there is a *tendency* in each direction, depending upon the personal attitude of the administrator towards the person. There are times when an administrator will feel compelled to make positive recommendations about those he personally dislikes, and negative recommendations about those he likes. Such cases will be in the minority, however, and will happen only when compelling reasons exist.

These small and minor exceptions to the rule do not invalidate the Basic Supposition. In fact, as exceptions, they merely serve to substantiate the rule. Some administrators even throw in such recommendations on occasion to prove how objective and fair-minded they actually are. Sophisticated administrators are able to give the appearance of making such seemingly contradictory recommendations when they, in reality, are following the dictates of the Basic Supposition. More likely than not, the recommendations and the personal likes and dislikes of the administrator will be in parallel. (*And keep in mind that "you never get a second chance to make a good first impression."* – Anon.)

Dr. Peter was alluding to the Basic Supposition when he stated that actions are often the result of "secret preferences based upon the personal likes, dislikes, and hidden values of those in power."[8]

Richard Armour was also attesting to the existence and use of the Basic Supposition in his interesting book entitled *Going Around in Academic Circles.* His illustration, although related to a faculty member assigning grades, demonstrates how a decision is often reached and then the data is only searched for the rationale and logic to support the recommendation.[9]

Armour relates the story of a relatively young professor who had the son of a wealthy trustee in his course in Analytic Geometry (which apparently gives little leeway for the use of subjectivity in grading). The student deserved a grade of C, but giving him an A would make a lot of people happy. The professor considered giving credit for neatness, but the student was very sloppy. Finally the young professor hit upon the basis for the A grade. Since the student knew more at the end of the semester than he did at the beginning, the basis of the grade would be *Improvement.* Thus, he gave the C student

[8]*The Peter Prescription,* Laurence J. Peter, William Marrow and Company, Inc., New York, New York, 1972, p. 94.
[9]*Going Around in Academic Circles,* Richard Armour, McGraw-Hill Book Company, New York, New York, 1965, p. 83.

an A, and prided himself on his personal knowledge that he was learning the academic ropes. (He had used the L.I.E. and B.S., although perhaps inadvertently.) This clearly illustrates that the data was not input to develop a recommendation (grade) but was only used to *develop a rationale* to justify the action.

Data (in the evaluation process) either speaks for itself or must be interpreted. Data speaks for itself when the recommendation and the data appear to be consistent (i.e., high performance ratings and a positive recommendation, or low performance ratings and a negative recommendation). Data must be interpreted when it appears on the surface to be inconsistent with the recommendations (i.e., high performance ratings and a negative recommendation, or low performance ratings and a posivite recommendation).

In such situations, the Agile Administrator interprets the data in an apparently logical and plausible manner which, not too surprisingly, fully supports the recommendation being made.

It will become patently clear that many recommendations are formulated long before data or information is evaluated, and that data is merely used to justify the recommendation already decided upon. The personal likes and dislikes of the administrator determined the recommendation, not the data.

Now, with this brief background on the Law of Inverse Evaluation and the Basic Supposition, let me introduce the main character of this book—the Agile Administrator.

1.3 THE AGILE ADMINISTRATOR (The A.A.)

"The Agile Administrator proceeds directly from an unwarranted assumption to a preconceived conclusion."
– Anon.

The Agile Administrator represents a composite characterization of all the *un*desirable traits which may be held by supervisors, managers, or administrators. Any resemblance to individuals you know, or have been exposed to, is purely *in*tentional. Unfortunately, the Agile Administrator exists and must be dealt with. He is defined in Exhibit 3, on the next page.

The Agile Administrator has the ability (and desire) to logically relate apparently inconsistent data and recommendations; that is, he can develop a completely logical explanation of why positive data can support a negative recommendation, and why negative data can sup-

---

EXHIBIT 3.
THE AGILE ADMINISTRATOR (The A.A.)[10]

An Agile Administrator is a person who is able to interpret all available data regarding performance and qualifications in such a manner that the interpretation will support either a negative or positive recommendation. He uses the Law of Inverse Evaluation in reaching his recommendations, and always operates under the Basic Supposition.[11]

---

port a positive recommendation.[12] An expert on the Law of Inverse Evaluation, he is capable of interpreting data in *polar extremes* and developing *logic* which supports his interpretation. Since his logic is plausible, his recommendations often get by without examination or scrutiny. This is a very important point. People are fooled into accepting the interpretation because the justification appears to be logical. (*"Logic is an instrument for bolstering a prejudice."* – Elbert Hubbard.)

The Agile Administrator (affectionately known as the Agile or A.A.) knows that others are always ready to *believe the worst about the best.* (*"There is always something about your success that displeases even your best friend."* – Oscar Wilde.) This knowledge permits him to perpetrate some real atrocities under the guise of personnel evaluation. When the data and the recommendation are consistent, no problem exists. But when the data is contrary to the recommendation (at least on the surface), then the Agile must bring his full range of ingenuity to bear on the situation. The predisposition to believe the worst about the best aids him in his efforts.

There is an infinite variety of forms in which data can be presented (i.e., percentages, charts, ratios, etc.), and the Agile Administrator is adept at choosing the form which presents the data in the manner which supports his recommendation. He realizes that few

---

[10]I do not wish to defame any organization by using the initials A.A. for the Agile Administrator, but in this day of using initials for everything, I really had no choice. ("Necessity is the argument of those who have no good reason." Anon.)

[11]I will be using the masculine "him" or "he" in referring to the Agile Administrator, realizing full well that there are female administrators fitting the description. I certainly do not wish to imply that there are no female Agile Administrators.

[12]The term *recommendation* means personnel actions such as promotions, salary changes, hirings, terminations, etc.

people will be able (or will wish) to read or analyze the material sufficiently to realize that it does not reflect the situation accurately. (*"Accuracy is the twin brother of honesty. Inaccuracy is the twin brother of dishonesty."* – Charles Simmons.) The strength of the Agile Administrator lies in the weaknesses of those with whom he deals. (*"All that is necessary for the triumph of evil is that good men do nothing."* – E. Burke.) He is confident that his recommendations will only receive hasty glances or cursory examination outside the area in which he operates. He counts on this lack of analysis as a means of perpetrating his deeds. He realizes that it is a relatively simple matter to hide behind the magic of numbers, if *in*sufficient information for a full interpretation of the material is given, or if it is presented in a manner that can be interpreted only as the Agile wishes it to be interpreted. This would seem that the Agile is "lying with statistics," but such need not be the case (although *it might be* the case). The Agile Administrator is capable of becoming a consummate, fluent, and devious liar. However, there is no need to do so, and intelligent administrators will not lie. The Law of Inverse Evaluation (the L.I.E.) permits them to avoid falsehoods in the name of personal interpretation. There is obviously a wide area for creativity in the personnel evaluation process.

Most Agile Administrators assume an air of objectivity, rather than subjectivity, in their personnel actions. Being objective has a positive connotation, whereas being subjective conjures up all kinds of negative impressions. On occasion, however, the Agile will claim that he is "forced" to take a subjective stance. He will use this technique when the action he is taking might be unpopular, or might meet with adverse reaction. This permits the Agile Administrator to make an unpopular recommendation while giving the appearance of not wanting to do so. Playing the role of Martyr is only one of the clever weapons in the Agile's arsenal. (*"A martyr* is anyone who is willing to sacrifice *others* for his own cause." – Elbert Hubbard.)

Of course no Agile Administrator will admit that most of his recommendations are based upon personal preferences and attitudes and may not reflect what is best for the particular person being evaluated or correct for the organization. (*"Agile Administrators exhibit behavior that is superficially correct, but intrinsically corrupt."* – Adapted from James Bryant Conant.) Just the opposite will be claimed. The Agile rationalizes that he is trying to strengthen the organization, not undermine it and its members. He tries to give the appearance that *he* is not taking any action at all, but is merely following what is dictated by the best interests of members of the firm. He is merely (he will claim) a slave to established policies. (*"Blindly following a policy is an easy substitute for thinking."* – Adapted from Ruth Smeltzer)

The Law of Inverse Evaluation is very applicable to *interpretation of* policies and procedures. There are equal and opposite ways for interpreting them, or deciding to accept or reject them. The Agile Administrator is able to accept or ignore existing policies with equal facility, and can develop the rationale to support either approach.

If he chooses to *use* an existing policy to support a recommendation or action, he merely defines his role (as an administrator) as being the one who insures that policies are enforced, despite personal preferences. (This usually means that he personally dislikes the policy but finds it useful to support his action.) On the other hand, should the Agile decide to *ignore* an existing policy or to make an exception, phrases such as "administrative discretion," "times have changed," "policies are rules, not gods," etc., are used to support his action. (Policy manuals, like the scriptures, can be interpreted to have said anything.)

This flexibility in the use or misuse of policies is particularly appropriate during the first year an administrator is in a position.[13] He *can accept* and use prior policies with justifications such as: "It is unfair to change the rules in mid-stream"; "I am bound by my predecessors"; "There is a need for continuity and stability"; etc. Or he can selectively *ignore* policies with such phrases as "I cannot afford to be bound by predecessors"; "I am now responsible"; "Times have changed"; "I did not create the policy and therefore do not feel committed to it"; "I must assess the situation on its particular [really, HIS] merits"; etc.

Nor need the Agile Administrator feel compelled to be *consistent* in interpretation or use of a policy at a later point in time (unless he thinks that it would be expedient to do so). (*"Consistency is the last refuge of the unimaginative."* – Oscar Wilde.) A ready rationale is available for taking an action which appears to be inconsistent with a prior stance on a policy or procedure. Based on a "seasoned viewpoint," "new and current information," "a better understanding of the organization and its people," etc., the Agile is "forced" to concede that his prior interpretation must be modified. Thus, the Agile Administrator continues to perpetuate the image of consistency and objectivity while remaining subjective and inconsistent. He is confident of pulling off his charade because he considers people outstandingly gullible and, in most cases, just plain naive. He is also aware that people are easily fooled by tenuous logic and distorted appearances

---

[13]Polar interpretation of policies further illustrates the broader applicability of the Law of Inverse Evaluation. This law is not confined to the personnel evaluation process, but can be (and is) used in politics, sports, and almost all aspects of life.

of reality. The Agile considers himself skillful at fooling people with inconclusive results and spurious logic. And he is relatively successful at doing just that. An Agile Administrator realizes that he can't fool all the people all the time, but he is content with a majority most of the time!

The use and abuse of deadlines (real or imagined) is another characteristic of the Agile Administrator. If the Agile wishes to *rush a recommendation* (to prevent anyone from mounting an offensive against his action), then he reasons that it is in the best interest of all parties to avoid unnecessary delays. If he *chooses to delay* action, then his rationale is that "personnel evaluations are serious matters which require lengthy deliberations; that it would be extremely unwise and unfair to rush pell-mell into such actions." Again, the Agile can rush or delay his recommendations with equally plausible logic to justify either approach.

Perhaps the most noticeable characteristic of Agile Administrators is their propensity for wanting criteria which are nebulous and ambiguous[14]—criteria which are readily succeptible to a full range of interpretations. This would be a covert desire, however, since on the surface the Agile would openly claim that he wanted, or had, objective criteria. (He is aware of the positive connotation associated with objectivity.) His overt actions could easily be misinterpretated by the uninformed as seeking criteria which could be uniformly applied and consistently interpreted. Beneath the surface, however, he is paying lip-service to developing such criteria. While giving the acceptable outward appearance of rejecting subjective criteria, he tries to project an image of being on an endless search (which, truthfully, will not end) for valid, objective criteria to use in the evaluation process. And now, let's talk about criteria.

1.4   CRITERIA FOR PERFORMANCE EVALUATION

"It is difficult to get an accurate measurement when you use a rubber yardstick." – Anon.

The Law of Inverse Evaluation and the Basic Supposition are at work in every organization in which employee performance is

---

[14]There is beauty in ambiguity! It is flexible, not rigid, not constraining, broad in scope, a guideline, not a god. It also is difficult to measure, too flexible, does not provide sufficient direction, is open to misinterpretation, etc. The Law of Inverse Evaluation explains why ambiguity can be interpreted in such ambiguous ways.

evaluated by managers, supervisors, or administrators. Business, government, and educational institutions all have their fair share of Agile Administrators who use the L.I.E. and B.S. in evaluating employees. The differences in performance evaluation among these three segments of society exist primarily in the specific criteria or standards used in the process. The kinds of actions taken as a result of such evaluations are similar: hiring, promoting, terminating, increasing or decreasing salaries, etc. Moreover, the two bases upon which all evaluations are (supposed to be) made are (1) performance on the job and (2) qualification for the position held or sought.

In order to present concrete illustrations of the operation of the B.S., the L.I.E., and the Agile Administrator, the academic environment was selected as the basis for this book. The major reason for this choice was that there are four well-defined and generally accepted criteria by which faculty members are judged (theoretically, at least), whereas in business and government there may be many criteria, all of which are ill-defined. It will be evident that the criteria used in academia give the illusion of being better defined than they actually are!

This section briefly defines the four areas in which faculty performance and qualifications are evaluated. The general applicability of these concepts to business and governmental agencies will be apparent from later discussions when specific details are given as to how the B.S. and L.I.E. are used in any evaluation process. (Having been involved with numerous business and governmental organizations over the past 25 years, I can personally attest to the general applicability of these concepts to all organizations in which performance is evaluated.)

The four criteria which are almost universally used in academia to evaluate performance and qualifications of faculty members are: (1) Teaching Effectiveness; (2) Research and Publications; (3) Professional Credentials, and (4) University/Community Contribution.

Faculty members are evaluated against these criteria at the time they are hired, and then annually for such personnel actions as promotions, salary increases, contract renewal, and tenure.[15] Only a brief

---

[15]*Tenure* in academia is similar to *seniority* in business and government. When a faculty member has been granted tenure (usually within 7 years of joining academia) he or she is guaranteed a job until retirement. During the pretenure years, performance reviews take place annually (similar to annual reviews in business and government) and either a contract is granted for the next year or the faculty member is terminated (a euphemism for fired).

Tenure is the ultimate goal in Academia, and those who have it jealously guard it!

definition of each criterion will be given here. Each one will be defined in the particular chapter devoted to it.

(1) TEACHING EFFECTIVENESS (The Teaching Criterion) refers to the ability of the professor to contribute to the learning process, whether learning actually takes place in the classroom or at other places or times. Evidence of such performance is usually gathered by student evaluations each year, which may or may not be published. Peer evaluations are sometimes used, but not as frequently as student evaluations.

(2) RESEARCH/PUBLICATIONS (The Research Criterion) represents the second most important (at least most frequently used) criterion for evaluating faculty performance. This category addresses scholarly output, represented by published articles, books, research papers, etc.

(3) PROFESSIONAL CREDENTIALS (The Credentials Criterion) refers to (a) degrees which have been achieved (terminal academic qualifications) or (b) equivalent experience and background. These two broad categories are called "academic" and "non-academic" credentials, respectively.

(4) UNIVERSITY/COMMUNITY CONTRIBUTION (The Contribution Criterion) covers those activities which require the faculty member to use his or her skills in the university community and within the larger society which is served by the university. This category is sometimes referred to as "professional development" and is closely related to the concept of "social responsibility" for businessmen and government officials.

Since there are four distinct criteria, some very obvious questions quickly come to mind: What is the relative weight given to each criterion? Are they all equally weighted, or is any one more important than any other? Must a faculty member be (fully) qualified in all four areas? Do educational institutions differ in their interpretations or uses of these criteria? Exhibit 4 attempts to address these related questions. (Watch the L.I.E. at work!)

Exhibit 4 presents six patterns to illustrate the wide range of interpretations placed upon the four criteria. Each criterion is depicted by a block, the size of which indicates the *relative weight* attached to that criterion with respect to the others. Obviously, the larger the block, the higher the relative importance of the criterion.

Assuming that each block could be one of three sizes (an infinite number of sizes actually exists) then there are 81 possible patterns.[16] Although I am certain that Agile Administrators have used all 81

---

[16]This total of 81 is arrived at by raising 3 (sizes) to the 4th (criteria) power.

possibilities and more, a brief explanation of these six patterns should provide the background for developing a logical explanation for the existence of any other pattern.

PATTERN NUMBER 1 (Four Large Blocks of Equal Size) represents the view held by new faculty members (and Agile Administrators when appropriate). Persons joining the academic community attempt to build credentials and performance in all four areas. This pattern also depicts the way in which some academic institutions would like others to think that they evaluate faculty members (demanding high quality performance in each criterion area), whereas pattern Number 6 might be a more accurate picture of the way the evaluation process is practiced (little is demanded in any area). A huge gap exists between what an organization *expects* from its members and what it actually receives and *accepts*.

PATTERN NUMBER 2 (The Teaching Block is Largest) shows the way faculty members who consider themselves good teachers (and Agile Administrators when appropriate) view the criteria. Students also view the criteria in this manner, concluding that the ability to teach is the most important aspect of faculty member performance.[17] This pattern illustrates a basic concept at work in any evaluation process in any organization: What we are good at (or think that we are) is, in our minds, the most important element in the evaluation process. What we are lacking is, obviously, of lesser importance. Viewed in this manner, it is little wonder that each person thinks that he or she should always receive favorable evaluations and positive recommendations.

PATTERN NUMBER 3 (The Research Block is Largest) represents the way research-oriented faculty members (and Agile Administrators when appropriate) view the four criteria. This pattern depicts the "publish or perish" environment for which academia is noted. New faculty members may see this pattern as the relative ranking of the four areas if they are receiving heavy pressure to publish.

PATTERN NUMBER 4 (The Credentials Block is Largest) is the view held by those faculty members who are lacking in the other three areas, and/or those who feel that their credentials are the strongest part of their backgrounds (and Agile Administrators when appropriate). This is the pattern claimed by all Agile Administrators who use the lack of a "terminal degree" (doctorate) to terminate faculty members.

PATTERN NUMBER 5 (The Contributions Block is Largest)

---

[17]Some students would eliminate the other three criteria entirely, leaving Teaching Effectiveness as the only criterion!

EXHIBIT 4.
The Relative Importance of TEACHING, RESEARCH, PROFESSIONAL CREDENTIALS and UNIVERSITY CONTRIBUTION as Viewed by Faculty Members, Students and Agile Administrators.

AS VIEWED BY:

New Faculty Members
and
Agile Administrators
when Appropriate. . .1

| TEACHING | RESEARCH | PROFESSIONAL CREDENTIALS | UNIVERSITY CONTRIBUTION |

Teaching Oriented
Faculty Members
and students and
Agile Administrators
when Appropriate. . .

| TEACHING | RESEARCH | PROFESSIONAL CREDENTIALS | UNIVERSITY CONTRIBUTION |

Research Oriented
Faculty Members
and
Agile Administrators
when Appropriate. . .3

| TEACHING | RESEARCH | PROFESSIONAL CREDENTIALS | UNIVERSITY CONTRIBUTION |

18

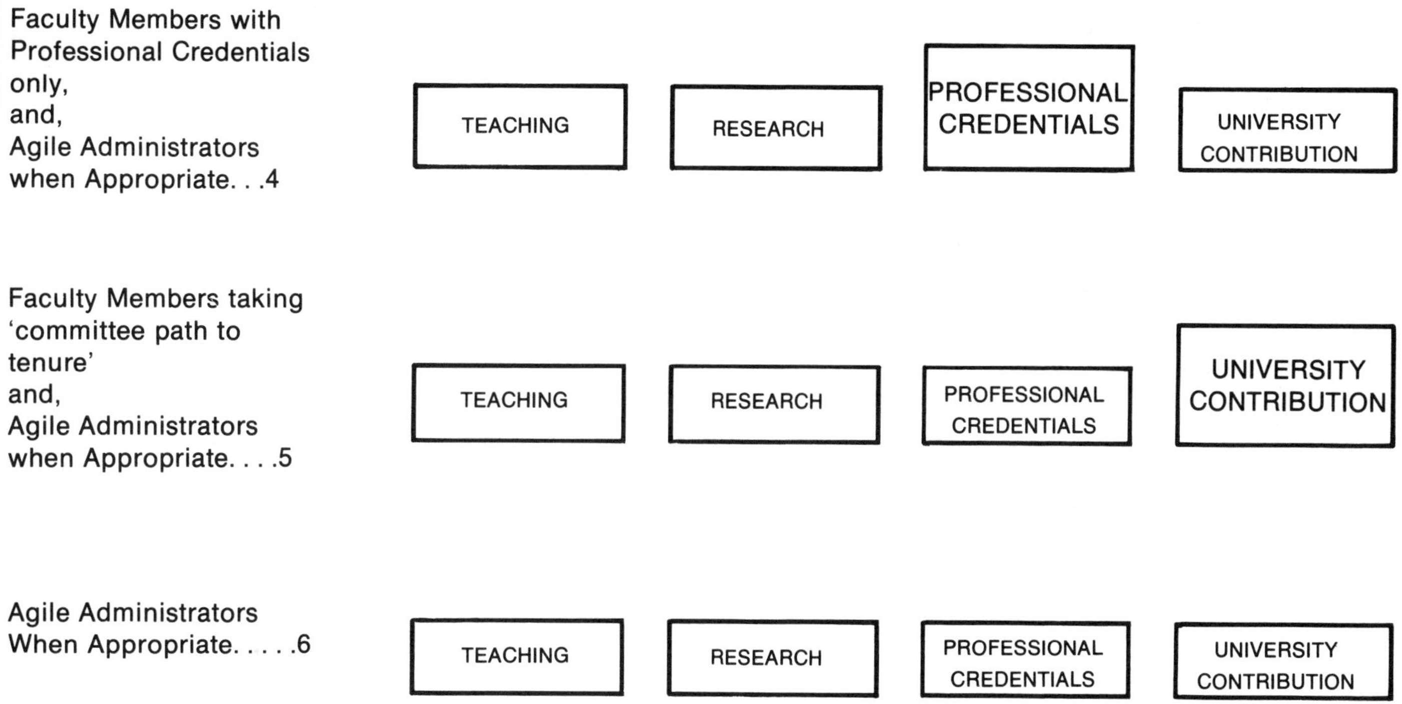

Faculty Members with
Professional Credentials
only,
and,
Agile Administrators
when Appropriate. . .4

TEACHING   RESEARCH   **PROFESSIONAL CREDENTIALS**   UNIVERSITY CONTRIBUTION

Faculty Members taking
'committee path to
tenure'
and,
Agile Administrators
when Appropriate. . .5

TEACHING   RESEARCH   PROFESSIONAL CREDENTIALS   **UNIVERSITY CONTRIBUTION**

Agile Administrators
When Appropriate. 6

TEACHING   RESEARCH   PROFESSIONAL CREDENTIALS   UNIVERSITY CONTRIBUTION

NOTE: The size of the block indicates the relative degree of importance attributed to that criterion. Other patterns are possible, but these are the most prevalent ones.

is used by faculty members who have taken the "committee route to tenure," or those who are not well qualified in the other three areas (and the Agile Administrator when appropriate). Those who rank the criteria in this pattern are actively involved in committee work within the institution and hope that this will lead to promotion and tenure.

PATTERN NUMBER 6 (Four Small Blocks of Equal Size) indicates that no criterion is more important than any other, and that all are *un*important. This is probably the actual pattern used in many academic institutions, while Pattern Number 1 would appear in all public relations material or the faculty manual. Faculty members who are not strongly qualified in any area (and Agile Administrators when appropriate) would use this pattern. This pattern is often used by the Agile Administrator when he wishes to hire one of his cronies who would not be qualified in *any* of the four areas.

Although an infinite number of patterns could be developed, these six are the most prevalent.[18] In the chapters which follow, each of the four criterion areas will be discussed at length; to illustrate how the Agile Administrator uses the Basic Supposition and the Law of Inverse Evaluation in formulating a pattern and constructing the logic which permits him or her to reach *any* recommendation with *any* data. First, let's look at the Teaching Criterion.

---

[18]To see how quickly the number of possible patterns rises, just allowing each block to take on four sizes (instead of three) increases the number of patterns to 256, from the original 81. (This is computed by raising 4 to the 4th power).

Average + Average + Average + Average = Below Average

2 Imparters of Knowledge

"Let thy speech be better than silence, or be silent."
— Dionysius the Elder.

"There are three good reasons for entering a teaching career—June, July, and August." — Anon.

"A university was defined by a Chinese student as an athletic institution in which a few classes were held for the feeble-minded." — Anon.

"Learning makes the wise wiser and the fool more foolish." — A Proverb.

2.0   IMPARTERS OF KNOWLEDGE

"Teaching is the art of making deep noises from the chest sound like important messages from the brain." – Adapted from H. I. Phillips.

This chapter addresses the method by which faculty members are evaluated for their effectiveness as teachers—as disseminators of knowledge.[1] This is not to imply that teaching effectiveness is the principal criterion for evaluating faculty members. Different institutions and administrations place varying weights upon the four criteria. However, since most institutions recognize the teaching obligation of faculty members, and this satire had to begin someplace, why not start with teaching effectiveness?

EXHIBIT 5 depicts the *generalized* wording that might appear in a faculty manual in order to define, in operational terms, what is meant by teaching effectiveness. This wording would serve as a guideline by which faculty members could be evaluated (or by which they assume they will be evaluated). It is evident in reading this exhibit that teaching effectiveness covers much more than performance in the classroom. However, in reality, classroom performance is generally the SOLE basis for evaluating teaching effectiveness.

Data on this performance is usually gathered by a questionnaire completed by students. The results of these surveys may or may not be published and distributed for general use each term, year, or semester.

Despite a wide range of opinions as to the validity and reliability of the data, student ratings of faculty performance are considered to be the best available evidence to evaluate teaching effectiveness.[2] After all, this data is quantified, and thus has *the mystique of quantification* to compensate for any lack of validity.

In the two sections that follow, it will be assumed that data exists from student-prepared ratings on the performance of the faculty member in the classroom. Should no data exist, the Agile Administrator is in an excellent position to make either a positive or negative

---

[1]"A professor is a person whose job it is to tell students how to solve the problems of life which he himself has tried to avoid by becoming a professor." Anon.

[2]At one institution, student evaluations were taken during the *third week* of a 14 week term, before even one-fourth of the class had been taught. In effect, students were asked to *anticipate* how effective the professor was *going to be* during the term.

EXHIBIT 5.
CRITERIA FOR EVALUATING TEACHING EFFECTIVENESS

This is a teaching institution, and as such, the quality of teaching will be the prime consideration in the selection, retention, promotion, and granting of tenure to faculty members. In order to assure a high quality level of teaching throughout the institution, it is desirable that faculty, students, and administrators have an annual assessment of teaching effectiveness for all full-time and part-time members of the faculty. Where possible and practical, peer group evaluations will also be used to evaluate and review faculty members.

Superior classroom performance is only one aspect of effective teaching, although a critical part of the evaluation process. Effective teaching also includes preparation for classroom performance and for the creation of an atmosphere that is conducive to learning and teaching. All forms of planned and unplanned faculty and student interaction, including the direction of student research and independent study, are considered as essential elements of teaching effectiveness.

Each faculty member is expected to contribute to the development of a stimulating atmosphere within the university community; that facilitates and encourages the learning process. Each faculty member should maintain regularly scheduled office hours, participate in student counseling, and be a visible presence on the campus during the normal term of the academic year. Each faculty member should assume, as a part of his/her teaching obligation, the promotion of and participation in a wide variety of activities which are designed to increase the amount of purposeful interaction between the faculty and the student body. Thus, teaching effectiveness, broadly defined, goes far beyond performance in the classroom.

recommendation. A positive posture would be justified on the basis that—in the absence of data to the contrary—it would be grossly unfair to assume anything but satisfactory performance in the classroom. A negative posture would, however, consider it inappropriate to make such an assumption, and the Agile would then interpret other criteria in a negative fashion. Or, the Agile could attend a class to see for himself—assuming that the professor agreed. Then the

Agile is in an excellent position to draw his preconceived conclusion from first-hand knowledge. Of course if the professor refused to permit him to attend the class, then only a negative connotation can be drawn from his refusal to cooperate.

A further assumption is that the data may be in Absolute Form, but could be placed in Trend Form if the faculty member has been rated by students over two or more time periods. Thus the Agile Administrator gets two cracks at the data . . . in Absolute Form or in Trend Form. This two-pronged attack provides enormous potential for the proper interpretation of data to justify either recommendation the A.A. wishes to make.

First, let's look at how the Agile Administrator evaluates Absolute Data.

2.1 USE OF ABSOLUTE DATA

"It appears that when statistics enter the scene,
common sense departs." – Darrell Huff.

Keep in mind that the Agile Administrator operates under the Basic Supposition, which states that he tends to make negative recommendations regarding faculty members whom he dislikes and positive recommendations for those who are in his favor. Also, the Law of Inverse Evaluation states that polar (opposite) interpretations exist for any piece of data on performance or qualifications. The Agile Administrator is one who is capable of both making such divergent interpretations and presenting the logic to make the data and the recommendation appear to be consistent, when (on the surface) there might be an apparent conflict between the two. With this brief review, let's proceed by developing the *six conditions* which can exist concerning absolute data on *teaching effectiveness*.

The form in which student evaluation data appears matters little; whether students responded to objective questions with answers ranging from 1 (poor) to 7 (excellent) or wrote subjective, narrative evaluations is unimportant.

There are three possible outcomes: (1) the data *appears* to rate the faculty member *above average* in teaching effectiveness, (2) the data *appears* to rate him *average,* or (3) the data *appears* to rate him *below average.*[3] Setting aside the difficulty of classifying the data as

---

[3]Whether the course is optional or required, quantitative or qualitative, hard or soft science, art or science is also ignored (if appropriate) by the Agile Administrator, or used to further interpret the data (if necessary).

above average, average, or below average (just more maneuvering room for the Agile Administrator), let's assume that these three outcomes are possible, and can be established for a given faculty member. Then there are *two conditions* which might exist *for each* of these three outcomes: that is, the faculty member is (a) liked or (b) disliked (not particularly liked) by the Agile Administrator. Therefore six possibilities occur:

1. Above Average ratings; faculty member is liked.
2. Above Average ratings; faculty member is disliked.

3. Average ratings; faculty member is liked.
4. Average ratings; faculty member is disliked.

5. Below Average ratings; faculty member is liked.
6. Below Average ratings; faculty member is disliked.

Exhibits 6, 7, and 8 summarize these six possibilities and give brief statements concerning the rationale and logic which the Agile Administrator might use in supporting either a positive or negative recommendation when the data is ABOVE AVERAGE, AVERAGE, or BELOW AVERAGE. It will become readily apparent that data is meaningless in the evaluation; that the only relevant factor is the personal likes or dislikes of the Agile Administrator.

Briefly, here is how the L.I.E. works for each of the six possibilities.

Above Average Teaching Ratings (Exhibit 6)

(1) Faculty Member is Liked (Positive Interpretation)
The Agile Administrator has no difficulty justifying a positive recommendation when the data is positive—the data speaks for itself in this case. (*"When data speaks for itself, be quiet."* – Anon.) High teaching ratings are an obvious indication of a good performer in the classroom; of a high quality teacher. And isn't this the best evidence on hand to make the evaluation? After all, who should know better than the students rating a course how effective a faculty member is? The Agile Administrator alludes to the fact that this is, after all, a teaching institution! So superior teaching must be recognized and rewarded; hence a positive recommendation for promotion, contract renewal, tenure, etc. (Note how ABOVE average becomes SUPERIOR teaching ratings when the latter word is used by the Agile in justifying his recommendation.)

EXHIBIT 6.
The L.I.E. in Operation: Evaluation of ABOVE AVERAGE Teaching Ratings

--Negative Interpretation--	++Positive Interpretation++
1. Faculty member is running a popularity contest. 2. Not demanding work from the students. 3. Teaching is only one aspect of the evaluation process. 4. Student ratings are suspect at best, invalid at worst. 5. Student evaluations are only a partial reflection of the teaching effectiveness of faculty members. 6. Effective teaching means more than classroom performance.	1. High student ratings are an indication of good teaching performance. 2. A high-quality teacher. 3. Teaching is the most important aspect of the evaluation process. 4. This is the best evidence we have to base an opinion upon. 5. Who should know better than the students what kind of teacher he/she is? 6. This is a teaching unit, and superior teaching performance should (must) be rewarded.

Should other criteria for this faculty member be less than satisfactory, then the Agile can either ignore such data (or at least not call attention to it) or define teaching as the principal criterion for positive recommendations. (The Criteria for Evaluating Teaching Effectiveness [Exhibit 5] certainly justifies such an interpretation!) In other words, teaching effectiveness becomes *the* criterion when student ratings are above average AND the Agile Administrator wishes to make a positive recommendation. (This ranking of the criteria reflects the second of the six patterns discussed in Chapter 1.)

(2) Faculty Member is Not Liked (Negative Interpretation)

Justifying a negative recommendation—non-renewal, no promotion, no tenure (tantamount to termination), etc.—is really not that difficult for the Agile Administrator. However, since the data does not speak for itself—that is, it appears to be contrary to the recommendation—some interpretation is needed. Quite obviously, a careful reading of the Criteria for Evaluating Teaching Effectiveness (Exhibit 5) makes it clear that classroom performance is *only one aspect* of teaching effectiveness. The issue is far more complex. Student evaluations are suspect at best, invalid at worst, so one must be careful not to put too much emphasis upon them.[4] Besides, student evaluations are only a partial reflection of the teaching effectiveness of the faculty ... other evidence is available (this can be said without elaboration). What appears to be happening, according to the Agile Administrator, is that the faculty member is not demanding any work from his students (hence, academic quality is dropping). The result, quite naturally, is high student ratings. Students don't like to work, and they appreciate faculty members who don't *make* them work. The faculty member is obviously running a popularity contest; therefore his students' ratings are meaningless. Other factors must therefore be considered. (Then the Agile proceeds to interpret—negatively, of course—the other criteria.

Average Teaching Ratings (Exhibit 7)

(3) Faculty Member is Liked (Positive Interpretation)

Since the ratings are not below average, it is a relatively straightforward matter for the Agile Administrator to justify a positive recommendation. The A.A. simply states that the ratings are NOT below average, or that the faculty member is NOT a bad teacher. Certainly average performance is acceptable. It would be flagrantly unfair to set a standard that required ABOVE average performance: this would invalidate the concept of an average. Not everybody can be above average. Of course, should other aspects of the faculty member's performance be above average, or interpreted thusly, these as-

---

[4]Students, unlike faculty, are transient members of the academic community and should not (according to the A.A.) have too much input into decisions about what faculty members will remain at the institution long after the students have graduated or left under other circumstances.

EXHIBIT 7.
The L.I.E. in Operation: Evaluation of AVERAGE
Teaching Ratings

− −Negative Interpretation− −	+ +Positive Interpretation+ +
1. Average Performance in the classroom is not enough. 2. Teaching effectiveness is only average. 3. This is a teaching unit, and we should expect more from our professors in the classroom. 4. This is the most important aspect of the evaluation process, and the record is not "above average."	1. Performance in the classroom is acceptable. 2. Teaching ratings are *not* below average. 3. This is a teaching unit, and the teacher is performing at an acceptable level. 4. There is certainly nothing negative about average teaching ratings. 5. (The research record could be cited as supporting a positive recommendation.) 6. (Teaching ratings could be ignored in the evaluation process.)

pects would be cited and probably highlighted as the overriding considerations for the positive recommendation. In fact the teaching ratings could be ignored, or simply taken for granted, and the Agile Administrator could base the positive recommendation on other information that might speak for itself more readily.

(4) Faculty Member is Not Liked (Negative Interpretation)
The teaching effectiveness criterion takes on a new dimension when

EXHIBIT 8.
The L.I.E. in Operation: Evaluation of BELOW AVERAGE Teaching Ratings

---Negative Interpretation---	++Positive Interpretation++
1. The data fully supports a negative recommendation. 2. The ratings indicate clearly that classroom performance is unacceptable. 3. Teaching is the most important aspect of the evaluation process, and the evidence is clearly negative. 4. This is a teaching unit, and below average performance in the classroom cannot be rewarded. 5. This is the best evidence we have to base an opinion upon. 6. Who should know better than the students what kind of teacher he/she is?	1. Quality is being demanded from the students, and they do not like it. 2. Students are trying to "get even" with the professor. 3. Students are in no position to judge the caliber of instruction they are receiving. 4. Student ratings are very suspect. 5. The data collection form is far from perfect. 6. (This aspect of the evaluation could be ignored.) 7. (Other aspects of the faculty member's qualifications and/or background could be cited.) 8. Teaching is only one aspect—not the most important—of the evaluation process. 9. The professor is obviously very scholarly and the students are not. 10. The faculty member is certainly not running a popularity contest.

the Agile Administrator dislikes a faculty member and the data is not very positive, which average (by definition) is not. Average performance in the classroom is not enough. This is a teaching institution and the most important function of the faculty member (for the present) is to perform in the classroom. Other aspects of teaching effectiveness mentioned in Exhibit 5 (Criteria for Evaluating Teaching Effectiveness) are not brought into the evaluation since they might be positive. Of course if they are negative then they become essential items in the evaluation and are used prudently. If other aspects of the faculty member's total contribution to the institution are negative (or easily interpreted to be so), the Agile Administrator uses the compound approach—stating that even though the faculty member is only average in the classroom, other aspects of his performance were the major factors leading to the negative recommendation. This is a general theme which will appear throughout the evaluation process: the A.A. highlights the positive side of the total contribution and ignores the negative when he wishes to make a positive recommendation, and highlights all negative factors while ignoring the positive factors when he wishes to make a negative recommendation.

Below Average Teaching Ratings (Exhibit 8)

(5) Faculty Member is Liked (Positive Interpretation)
The data and the recommendation appear to be contradictory but this is only a figment of the imagination. The logic and rationale to support a positive recommendation based upon negative data are readily available. The Agile Administrator simply justifies a positive recommendation when teaching ratings are below average by, in effect, invalidating the entire student rating process (for this particular faculty member) or by de-emphasizing this criterion. Obviously, according to the Agile, this faculty member is demanding scholarly performance from students and they don't like it. The faculty member is scholarly but the students are not. They are trying to get even with the faculty member by giving him poor teaching ratings. Besides, students are in no position to judge the caliber of the teaching they are receiving. They need a few years out in the real world to properly assess the performance of the faculty member and the material covered in class. This faculty member is certainly not running a popularity contest (to his credit), and is trying to extract performance from students. Naturally his ratings will suffer. That is to be expected. And student ratings are far from perfect. (Of course, the Agile Administrator could totally ignore this criterion in evaluating this faculty member, relying upon the other three criteria if one or more of them

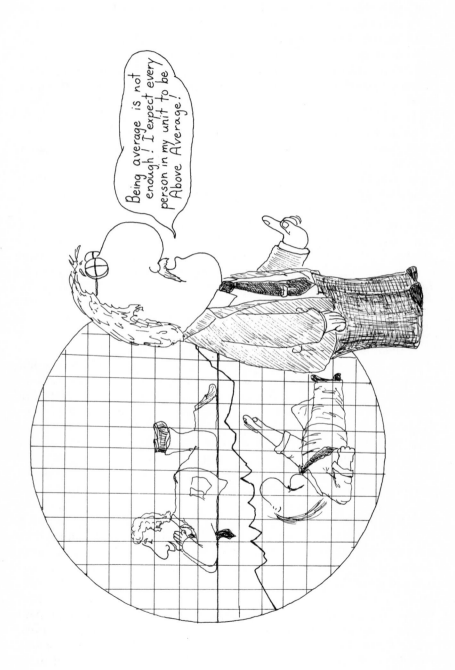

can more easily be interpreted as positive. Should all criteria be negative, and the Agile Administrator still wish to make a positive recommendation, then little justification would be forwarded with the recommendation: as little as he could get away with.) After all, there are four criteria and this is only one of them. An administrator must look for a *total pattern of contribution*—not every one (any one?) of the criteria has to be above average.

(6) Faculty Member is Disliked (Negative Interpretation)
With poor teaching ratings and an administrator who dislikes him, the faculty member can expect a negative recommendation. It is so easy to let the data speak for itself. On the surface the data and the recommendation are consistent; thus, no interpretation or justification is needed. The Agile Administrator cites poor teaching ratings as the basis for the negative recommendation. After all, the least we can expect from the faculty in a teaching institution is average performance in the classroom. Since this is the best available evidence, a negative recommendation certainly seems justified. And who should know better than students who are rating the professor whether he is performing well at the function of imparting knowledge in the class? Besides, the faculty manual is very clear on the subject: teaching effectiveness is the principal criterion for evaluating faculty members. (Stating that something is "very clear" is a dead giveaway that the item is not clear but the interpreter wishes to convey the impression that only one logical interpretation is possible.) Thus, since both the recommendation and the data are negative, the Agile Administrator is on secure grounds. The logic of the recommendation appears to be sound. Should other aspects of the faculty member's performance also be negative, these would be brought into the evaluation process. Positive criteria would, of course, be ignored or underemphasized.[5] When a criterion is below average, and the Agile Administrator dislikes the faculty member being evaluated, that criterion somehow becomes the most important one of the four.

---

[5]A few minor positive statements might be made in the recommendation. By sprinkling in a few good points with the bad, the Agile gives the appearance of objectivity in his evaluation. (*"A little truth helps a lie go down."* – Italian Proverb.)

High Teaching Ratings may be interpreted as high performance in class or low performance demands!

2.2   USE OF TREND DATA

"A well-presented figure is better than a flagrant lie, and just as effective. It misleads and distorts reality, but is presented in such a logical fashion that no misdeed can be pinned on you." – Darrell Huff.

Up to this point we have only been discussing the uses of Absolute Data in evaluating teaching effectiveness. There still exists the whole realm of Trend Data which might enter into the evaluation process. And it will, if the absolute data is not sufficient to justify the recommendation being made by the Agile Administrator, or if additional supporting data is needed. Knowing that both absolute and trend data can be used gives the A.A. an additional measure of flexibility in the evaluation process.

Many sophisticated techniques have been developed for getting data to project exactly what you want it to. It is not my purpose to discuss these techniques in any detail, only to suggest that trend data (as well as absolute data) may seem to imply many things to many people—largely depending on how the material is presented, and how it is initially interpreted.[6] When you know what you want the data to show, the technique for presentation is available to assist you.

Generally speaking, there are three basic trends that can be detected: (1) an UPWARD trend, (2) a DOWNWARD trend, and (3) a CONSTANT trend.[7] Then there are three variations of each of these trend lines, giving nine possible patterns of trend data to evaluate or use:

An UPWARD Trend:

1. Beginning and Ending Above Average
2. Beginning Below Average and Ending Above Average
3. Beginning and Ending Below Average

---

[6]Many of these techniques are well illustrated in *How to Lie With Statistics,* referenced in the Bibliography. Most Agile Administrators have probably read this book, but those being evaluated should also be aware of its contents—for self protection, of course.

[7]There is an infinite variety of patterns, with various peaks and valleys. These basic patterns have been smoothed.

A DOWNWARD Trend:

4. Beginning and Ending Above Average
5. Beginning Above Average and Ending Below Average
6. Beginning Below Average and Ending Below Average

A CONSTANT Trend:

7. Beginning and Ending Above Average
8. Beginning and Ending on the Average Line
9. Beginning and Ending Below Average

These nine basic trend patterns are illustrated in EXHIBIT 9.

The flexibility of nine trend lines, either absolute or trend data, and four criteria areas for the total evaluation process all give the Agile Administrator ample opportunity to pick and choose how he will justify his recommendations—all illustrating the fertile field for imagination and innovation which is embodied (embalmed?) in the evaluation process.[8]

EXHIBIT 9 is a *simple* illustration of the use of line charts. This is only one of many ways in which material can be presented. (For more details, see Chapter 5, *How to Lie with Statistics.*) With equal honesty or dishonesty a chart can be chosen and the data presented in such a fashion that the only logical conclusion that can be drawn is one which supports the recommendation of the Agile Administrator. Why else would the A.A. have chosen that method (among others) to present the data? Certainly not in the interest of an unbiased presentation of the facts.

Using the Basic Supposition and the Law of Inverse Evaluation, each one of the nine basic trend patterns can be interpreted in a negative or positive fashion.[9] It would serve no useful purpose, and would be very redundant, to discuss how each of the patterns could be interpreted in both a negative and a positive manner. After all,

---

[8]Keep in mind that opportunities for presenting and interpreting qualifications and credentials are available to those being evaluated too!

[9]Of course, data can also be interpreted in the neutral sense of being unable to ascertain if a trend exists, or of having insufficient time to detect any trend, etc. Such interpretations can be useful if the obvious trend would be contrary to the recommendation being made.

EXHIBIT 9.
THE NINE BASIC PATTERNS OF TREND DATA

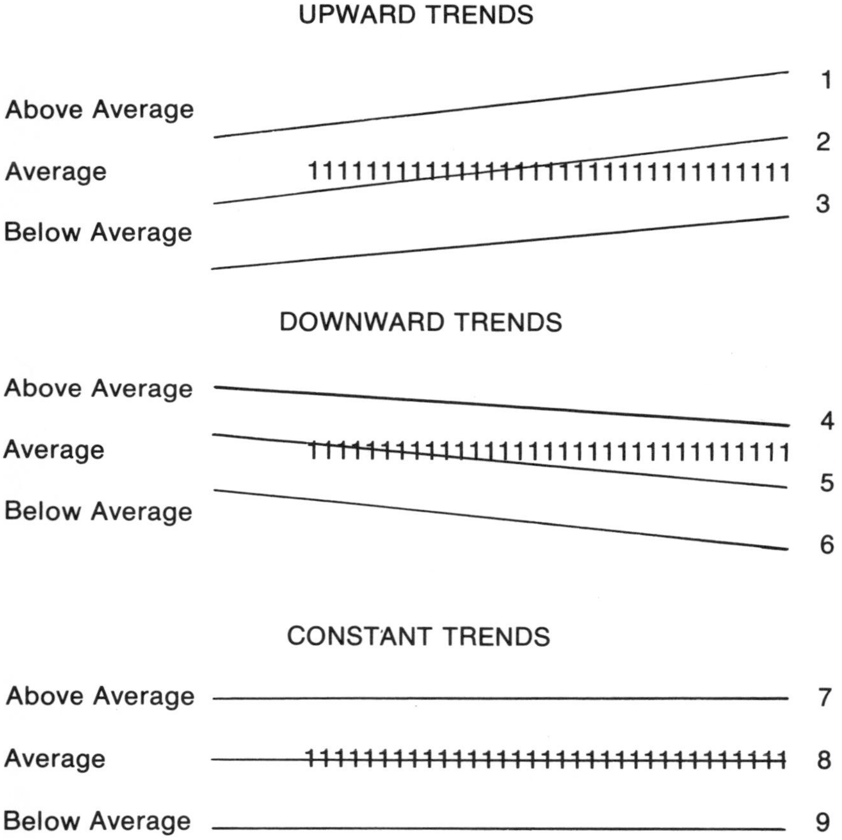

UPWARD TRENDS

Above Average

Average 11111111111111111111111111111111

Below Average

1
2
3

DOWNWARD TRENDS

Above Average

Average 11111111111111111111111111111111

Below Average

4
5
6

CONSTANT TRENDS

Above Average ———————————— 7

Average —11111111111111111111111111111111— 8

Below Average ———————————— 9

NOTE: The horizontal axis represents time periods (selected by the preparer of the charts) which might represent semesters, terms, academic years, etc. As mentioned, there is probably an infinite number of patterns with peaks and valleys. These nine basic patterns have been smoothed.

something must be left to the imagination. Perhaps illustrating a few of these patterns will demonstrate how the Agile can interpret the same trend in diametrically opposite ways.

Upward Trend, *Line 1,* Starting and Ending Above Average.

Positive Interpretation: The A.A. indicates that the trend is upwards (implicitly stating that this is good, positive, etc.) and that the absolute data is above average.[10]

Negative Interpretation: The A.A. ignores the trend (does not prepare the chart) and interprets the absolute data as supporting his contention that the faculty member continues to run a popularity contest in class and/or that teaching ratings are suspect anyway.

After all, the faculty member must be doing something that the students like, since he continues to get increasing ratings, and that can't possibly be demanding performance from students.

Downward Trend, *Line 4,* Starting and Ending Above Average.

Positive Interpretation: The A.A. would not prepare this trend chart because on the surface it implies a decline in teaching effectiveness with the downward slope. He would cite the absolute data instead, since it is above average. (This case illustrates an example where the absolute data and the trend data apparently are saying different things, if the data is left to speak for itself. This suggests that having a good year in student ratings can present problems in the subsequent year, since a downward trend is highly probable, with attendant negative implications.)

Negative Interpretation: A downward trend just seems to imply deterioration, or other negative connotations. "There appears to be a serious deterioration (decline) in the performance of the faculty member in the classroom" might be cited. (However, the Agile would not indicate or acknowledge that even at the bottom of the trend line the data is still *above average!*) This trend line is particularly useful to

---

[10]Some faculty members have influenced their student ratings by reading the evaluation forms and strategically timing appropriate comments (using buzz words from the form) just prior to the time the forms are completed. Another method is to get an average year in terms of ratings, and then use appropriately timed remarks to show marked improvement in teaching effectiveness. Those on multi-year contracts find it advisable take a long term view and insure that their ratings rise each year, then use this as their case for contract renewal, promotion, or tenure.

the Agile if a good faculty member had a particularly high rating one year, since the next year will probably be *lower*—but not necessarily *low*. Then the trend line could be cited as "a serious deterioration which portends a real problem in the future," thereby fully supporting a negative recommendation.

Constant Trend, *Line 7,* Starting and Ending Above Average.
Positive Interpretation: "There has been a consistent pattern of teaching effectiveness which is above the average of the unit." Or, "there is a continuous pattern of teaching effectiveness that is *well above* average." Such a statement is only a subjective interpretation as to how high above average the trend line actually is.
Negative Interpretation: "There has been no (noticeable) improvement (implying that improvement is necessary) in teaching performance over the time period covered by the trend line." Of course, it will not be stated that the absolute data (upon which the trend line is based) is all above average. Here, the appearance of a horizontal line seems to imply a lack of improvement or other negative connotations.

Constant Trend, *Line 9,* Starting and Ending Below Average.
Positive Interpretation: Here the trend line can easily be interpreted in a neutral or positive manner. "A consistent pattern of teaching effectiveness" or "no decline in performance in the classroom" might be the phrases used to justify a positive recommendation.
In this case the use of trend data is a little better (for whom?) than the use of absolute data. The below average situation would be fairly obvious with the absolute data, but is concealed by using a constant (horizontal) trend line.
Negative Interpretation: Here the absolute data (since it is all below average) would be the better route to go to support the negative recommendation since it would speak for itself. However, the trend line would be thrown in to further illustrate that there has been "no improvement in teaching effectiveness" over the time period covered by the data. Besides, a horizontal line seems to say that progress is missing, since a rising line on such a chart implies growth, progress, improvement, etc.

These few illustrations have really only touched the surface of the multifold possibilities for the use of trend data. I have not mentioned the various means for influencing the structure of the chart, such as what scale to use, what time periods to include (or exclude), what data to use, etc. Nor have I mentioned the real or implied assumptions which could seriously be challenged, but which are usually not presented by the Agile preparing trend charts: (1) the trend will continue in the same fashion, and (2) all other things being equal (which they usually are not). The trend to this point in time may be a "fact" (whatever that is), as viewed by the preparer of this chart, but any extension or extrapolation of this trend is definitely an opinion of the chartmaker. A facile mind, combined with the techniques for presentation which are available and acceptable, can devise any chart to say anything the Agile Administrator (or anyone else) wishes to say.

There may be situations in which positive trend data has been submitted *by the faculty member* as justification for suggesting a positive recommendation (tenure, contract renewal, promotion), yet the Agile Administrator wishes to (and will) make a negative recommendation. This presents no problem, since the logic is readily available to bind together the positive trend and the negative recommendation. It goes somewhat like this:

> "Although trends are useful indicators over time, decisions must be made in the present. Therefore, although not ignoring such trends, and keeping them in mind as they might affect future decisions (recommendations), present decisions must be based upon data which is in hand, not which may be available in the future. There is no assurance that the trend will, in fact, continue. Further, it is premature (sounds negative, doesn't it?) to conclude that a trend has been established, one that can reasonably be expected to continue into the future."

Thus, the Agile Administrator ignores the favorable trend and uses this logical explanation to justify his subjective (he will call it objective) recommendation. (*"The narrower the mind, the broader the statement."* – Ted Cook.)

However, should the trend give even a light glimmer of being positive, and the Agile wishes to make a positive recommendation based upon the trend, it is equally easy for him to develop a rationale which permits a current interpretation and extrapolation of the trend that could certainly not be defended upon any but the most subjective grounds. The L.I.E. continues to be supported; polar interpretations are plausible, and the A.A. is capable of reaching and justifying either pole with equal facility.

2.3 SUMMARY STATEMENTS

1. Different institutions and different administrators place different emphasis upon different criteria.

2. Data that is quantified has the mystique of quantification to make up for any lack of validity or consistency.

3. If absolute data cannot be interpreted to support a recommendation (an unlikely prospect) then trend data can, and vice versa.

4. The logic exists to combine positive data and negative recommendations, or negative data and positive recommendations.

5. When data speaks for itself, the Agile Administrator often keeps quiet.

6. The Agile Administrator is able to fool people with his recommendations because the logic he uses seems so plausible.

7. A well-presented figure is better than a flagrant lie, and just as effective.

8. Techniques have been developed that will permit one to get data to imply or infer exactly what one wants it to.

9. Having both absolute and trend data to use gives the Agile Administrator more flexibility in the personnel evaluation process.

10. Trend data may appear to display exactly the opposite of the absolute data which was used to prepare the trend line.

11. Upward trend lines imply positive notions; downward trend lines imply negative notions; horizontal trend lines imply neutral notions. And *all* may be misleading.

12. Data can be presented in such a form that only one logical conclusion emerges.

13. Having a good year in terms of student ratings could present a problem for the faculty member being evaluated, since ratings must drop the next time, or at least not increase.

14. A facile mind, combined with the techniques of data presentation, can devise any chart to say anything.

15. Teaching effectiveness can be interpreted to be either the most important of the four criteria or the least important.

3   Seekers of the Truth

"Good imitation is the most perfect originality."
– Voltaire.

"A new thinker, when studied closely, is merely a person who does not know what other people have thought."
– Frank Moore Colby.

"His wife not only edited his works but edited him too."
– Van Wyck Brooks.

"Some books are lies from end to end."
– Robert Burns.

3.0   SEEKERS OF THE TRUTH

"Research is an organized method of finding out what you are going to do when you can't keep on doing what you are doing now." – Charles F. Kettering.

While interviewing a prospective candidate for a faculty position, the author asked him why he had left his previous position. His answer was short and to the point. "I was in a publish or perish environment, and I perished." (*"This young man turned to me with a disarming candor which instantly put me on guard."* – Adapted from H. H. Munro [Saki].) While such candor is noticeably lacking in candidates for faculty positions, the reason many faculty members are transient was well stated by that young man. Publish or perish environments do exist, despite hues and cries to the effect that "this is not a publish or perish environment." (*"To Publish or Perish. That is the Academic Question."* – Anon.) Therefore, it is no surprise that Research/Publications is one of the four criteria by which faculty members are evaluated. This chapter shows how that evaluation takes place when the Agile Administrator, working under the Basic Supposition, uses the Law of Inverse Evaluation.

EXHIBIT 10 presents a description of the Research/Publication criteria as it might appear in a typical faculty manual. Notice how a publish or perish environment is immediately denied (since that is the appropriate thing to say) while the rest of the description leaves little doubt that faculty research and publication are expected. As the description is worded, it is completely acceptable for the Agile Administrator to recommend termination for lack of scholarly publications, or to grant tenure with absolutely no research or publications to the faculty member's credit.[1] Both recommendations, although they are opposite in nature, are consistent with the faculty manual.

This criterion may cause more negative recommendations (non-renewal, non-promotion, non-tenure) than the other three areas combined. For one thing, it is easy to use. If there are no publications, this is an obvious situation and this criterion is used as the basis for a negative recommendation. On the other hand, having a multitude

---

[1] At one institution, one faculty member was denied a promotion with two books and over two dozen publications of all kinds, while another faculty member within the same unit (and at the same time) was granted tenure with absolutely no publications whatsoever. The basis for the negative recommendation for promotion was a lack of *adequate* publications; yet, having *no publications* did not interfere with a positive recommendation for tenure.

of publications does not guarantee that this criterion will be considered met. How, then, are publications evaluated to see if this criterion is being met?

Research/Publications (according to the faculty manual description outlined in Exhibit 10) must be "significant and substantial scholarly contributions." What is *significant?* What is *Substantial?* What is *scholarly?* What is a *contribution?* Having four such nebulous words in the faculty manual insures that any interpretation can be placed upon the research and publication efforts of the faculty. Yet, this is exactly the type of wording found in many faculty manuals.

**EXHIBIT 10.
CRITERIA FOR EVALUATING RESEARCH AND PUBLICATIONS**

This university does not subscribe to a "publish or perish" environment. However, it is recognized that there is no inherent conflict between effective teaching and active participation in research. A superior teaching faculty will enhance its teaching and study with scholarly activities which might result in publications and research, and that expand the field of knowledge in the faculty member's area of training, education, and experience. Each faculty member should actively participate in some form of scholarly research. Evidence of such participation would be the creation of significant and substantial scholarly contributions which could reasonably be expected to appear in the leading journals in the faculty member's field of expertise. Such research and publications will attempt to demonstrate a sincere and concerned effort toward advancing the general level of knowledge in the faculty member's field of knowledge.

Research and Publications are often evaluated on the basis of the journal in which they appear; the number of pages published; the title of the publication; the quantity of publications one has; but seldom on the substantive content of the material (with, admittedly, rare exceptions). Other criteria for judging the scholarliness of research and publications include the size of the bibliography (and whether it includes any references to the administrator making the evaluation) and the number (and length) of footnotes.[2]

---

[2]'Footnotes are an abomination!' Huber Elliott.

Increasing the "scholarliness" of a publication by the judicious sprinkling of a few footnotes!

You will notice a large number of strategically located footnotes throughout this book. Since the scholarly rating of any publication is directly related to the number of footnotes (and I am in academia), a sprinkling of footnotes reeks with scholarliness. Ob Cit-ing and Ibid-ing are both excellent ways to increase the scholarly aura of footnotes.

Of course, sesquipedalian jargon (using large words, for the uninformed) enhances the scholarly content of a publication. Exhibit 11 illustrates how a simple memo can be brightened by the judicious use of a few well-chosen words. This is an actual memo that was prepared and sent by the author to someone who liked to spice up memos with unnecessarily long and esoteric words. As Edgar Allen Poe once said: "There lives no man, who at some period has not been tormented by an earnest desire to tantalize a listener by circumlocution."

Is it a significant, substantial contribution if you are able to get people to understand and utilize knowledge, or must you contribute *new information* to the field? Must the audience for the research/publication be scholars, or could it be practitioners who might use the knowledge?[3] Is it a significant contribution to explain the complex in terms which the layman can understand? Or, is only *newly created knowledge* what is meant by a significant and substantial contribution to the literature? Obviously, these questions will not be answered in any definitive fashion, since that would reduce the flexibility for wide-ranging interpretations of the criterion.

And now, let's peek in on the Agile Administrator interpreting the research and publication criterion in faculty personnel actions. First we will look at how *Absolute Data* is evaluated, and then we shall look at how *Trend Data* is evaluated, following a format similar to that used to evaluate teaching effectiveness in Chapter 2.

3.1   EVALUATING ABSOLUTE DATA

"Writing is the art of applying the seat of the pants to the seat of the chair." – Mary Heaton Vorse.

Whether one engages in research and publications or not may have little or no positive benefits for the faculty member! It may also be irrelevant whether your publications are widely sold (circulated,

---

[3]One administrator concluded that a hardback published book *did not* fall within the Research/Publication criterion because it had been written (according to the administrator) to be of practical use!

EXHIBIT 11.
SAMPLE OF A SCHOLARLY MEMORANDUM

TO: Esteemed Colleague   Anno Domini: Contemporaneous
IN RE: Grandiose Memoranda

Circumlocutionary memoranda inextricably intermingled with superfluous and supercilious verbiage connote psychic ineptitude, per se. Sesquipedalian jargon of esoteric origin and utility militates interpersonal comprehension.

Since self-abnegation denies adequate overt expression, it appears banal and hackneyed to loquacious individuals. Ostentatiousness, conversely, necessitates puerile undulations of the cerebellum. Incohesiveness dominates the tome. Diaphanous and tenuous conclusions alternately emerge. The communicative process looms ephemeral to all except the most perspicacious. Clairvoyant, phlegmatic effort is consummated by spurious admonitions, as obfuscate unintelligibility permeates the grandiloquent epistle. Even consummate philologists, erudite in lexicographic and etymological utilization, seek illuminating clews in magniloquent interlocution.

Recapitulatory vituperations irascibly predominate solitary soliloquys. Cognitive abracadabra finds germane immateriality in omnipotent effusion. Iconoclastic interlocution parallels cryptographic laconicism. Innuendos portending panaceas for egregious insufficiency of scintillating correspondence engender literary ostracism. Egocentricity substitutes plebeian, mundane parameters for scholarly verbosity. The gauntlet is haughtily epitomized by subsequent palavers. Euphonious polysyllabic pomposity ignominiously mulcts the ingenuous. Cacophony previals in lieu. Consequently, anachronistic memoranda achieve antipathy.

Nom de plume

GRA/pf

used) or not distributed at all. The key variable (of course) in the evaluation of absolute data on research/publications hinges upon whether the administrator doing the evaluation likes you or not. If you are liked, then your record of publications will be adequate. If you are disliked, then you will probably fall short in the criterion.

Exhibits 12, 13, and 14 summarize the polar interpretations of three categories of research/publication: (1) below average, (2) average, or (3) above average amounts. Of course, these are three relative and subjective categories, and there are shades of each one. But for the sake of argument, let's assume that these are three discreet categories into which all faculty publication and research records can be classified. Then, each faculty member is either (1) liked or (2) disliked. This establishes six situations which might exist as research and publications are evaluated. We will briefly explore these conditions, and the Agile's thinking, as he *sifts through the data* toward the ultimate conclusion reached before the data was even gathered.[4]

Below Average Research Publications (Exhibit 12)

(1) Faculty Member is Liked (A Positive Recommendation)
The Agile Administrator justifies his/her positive recommendation by stressing that this is not a publish or perish environment. It matters little whether this is a true statement. It does present a plausible rationalization for the positive recommendation when the data appears to be negative. Students should find no fault with this recommendation, *if* this faculty member happens to get favorable teaching ratings (at least not flagrantly bad ones). Or, the Agile could look at other aspects of the faculty member's performance or qualifications and highlight those which are positive, or easily interpreted to be so.

If there has been even a little research/publication, then quality can be stressed. ("When quantity is missing, stress quality. When quality is missing, stress quantity. When both are missing, stress other criteria.") Or the point could be made that there is a need to maintain a balance in proportions of teachers and researchers on the staff, since both contribute to the overall quality of the education students are receiving. "Good teachers cannot be sacrificed on the altar of research" might be the battle cry of the Agile Administrator. "Excel-

[4]The pattern of interpretation using the L.I.E. should be rather obvious at this point. Thus, those who are familiar with the pattern and process may wish to peruse the remainder of this chapter at a rapid pace. Additional illustrations are presented in some detail for those who wish to master the concept completely.

EXHIBIT 12.
The L.I.E. in Operation: Evaluation of a BELOW AVERAGE Research/Publications Record

−−Negative Interpretation−−	++Positive Interpretation++
1. Not enough publications and/or research.	1. Quality is evident, although quantity is not high.
2. Does not meet this criterion.	2. This is only one criterion.
3. Although this is not a "publish or perish unit," etc.	3. This is not the critical criterion.
4. Fails to meet the standard.	4. This is a teaching unit, and we are expected to be teachers, not just researchers.
5. We have too many faculty members who have not published, and we can't be burdened with more.	5. This criterion is not appropriate for this particular case.
6. This criterion is critical.	6. Not everyone can be a prolific researcher.
7. This criterion is critical in this case.	7. We need to keep a small number of faculty members who might not publish a lot.

lent teachers, not isolated researchers" might also be a useful phrase to slip into the positive recommendation. The Agile Administrator will maintain that he is defending the students' rights to keep a good teacher and not letting such a small item as limited (don't say non-existent) research and publications interfere with the retention of those faculty who are an asset to the institution.

The Agile has to be careful that he doesn't get carried away in the rationale for his positive recommendation when this criterion clearly is not being met—it might arouse suspicion. However, a little hyperbole can go a long way towards clouding the issue.

(2) *Faculty Member Disliked* (A Negative Recommendation)
The Agile Administrator begins the justification for the negative recommendation in the same manner as he did for the positive recommendation, namely: "This is not a publish or perish environment."
But then he proceeds to state that it is obviously expected that faculty
members will contribute to the scholarship of their fields, no matter
how little that contribution might be. (This last phrase is dropped if
the faculty member has a few publications, but is frequently used if
there are none.) Therefore, this faculty member (not in the favor of
the A.A.) has not fulfilled the contractual obligation as clearly outlined in the faculty manual. The A.A. therefore *has no choice,* and is
forced to take the only course open to him—making a negative recommendation on contract renewal, promotion, tenure, etc.[5]

"Being forced to take the only course of action" is a favorite
phrase of the Agile Administrator. Making reluctant decisions gives
the overt appearance of trying to be fair, impartial, unbiased, objective, honest, etc., while all the time implementing personal recommendations based upon personal likes and dislikes and completely
ignoring the criteria spelled out in the faculty manual.

The Agile Administrator might quote directly from the faculty
manual on the Research/Publication criterion, to lend an air of scholarliness to the recommendation (and, indirectly, to interpret it for
any person or group that might be reviewing the recommendation).

But what if the manual is silent on the issue of research and
publication, and the Agile Administrator wishes to use this criteria as
the basis for a negative recommendation? No problem! It takes little
imagination or ingenuity to assume that this is *implied* in the manual,
or that the requirement was so *obvious* (and such a recognized part
of faculty member performance and qualifications) that the faculty
manual did not belabor the point. The A.A. continues the negative
recommendation with the interpretation of the manual that was apparent for him (which, since the faculty member was disliked, had to
be negative).

Now we'll see what happens if the faculty member has published
what has been subjectively determined to be an Average amount.
How can this be interpreted in diametrically oppsoing ways?

---

[5]"The modern politician perpetuates the same instinct when he explains,
however unconvincingly, that he is only the instrument of his constituents,
the expression not of his own preferences but of the public good." John
Kenneth Galbraith, *Economics and the Public Purpose,* Houghton Mifflin Company, Massachusetts, 1973.

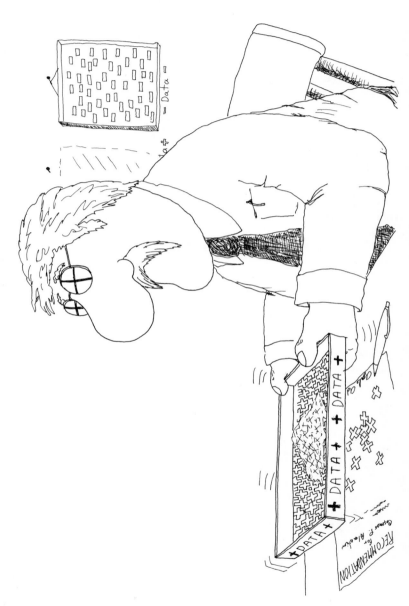

Sifting through the data to find the rationale for the recommendation which has been made!

AVERAGE RESEARCH /PUBLICATIONS (Exhibit 13)

(3) Faculty Member is Liked (A Positive Recommendation)
The Agile Administrator has little difficulty in justifying a positive recommendation on the research/publications criterion when the faculty member has at least an average amount of research to his/her credit. If other aspects of the faculty member's performance are marginal, then the Agile Administrator might go to great lengths to build up the research/publication contribution of the faculty member. The A.A. could personally assess the publications to lend credence to the recommendation. Or the Agile could refer to the editorial board which approved the publications, if one were used—implying (or boldly stating) that the material must have been a contribution since that august board accepted the material for publication. Or if the research/publication was funded, then it must have been of obvious value to attract a sponsor who was willing to finance the project. It

---

EXHIBIT 13.
The L.I.E. in Operation: Evaluation of an AVERAGE Research/Publications Record

––Negative Interpretation––	++Positive Interpretation++
1. Not enough publications.	1. Not Below Average.
2. Average is not enough.	2. Average is sufficient to meet this criterion.
3. More quantity needed.	3. Quality is high, although quantity is average.
4. Does not meet the criterion of contribution to the field.	4. This is a teaching unit.
5. More quality is needed.	5. Publication is only one aspect of the evaluation process.
6. Research/publications is a very important one of the criteria.	6. This is not a publish or perish environment.

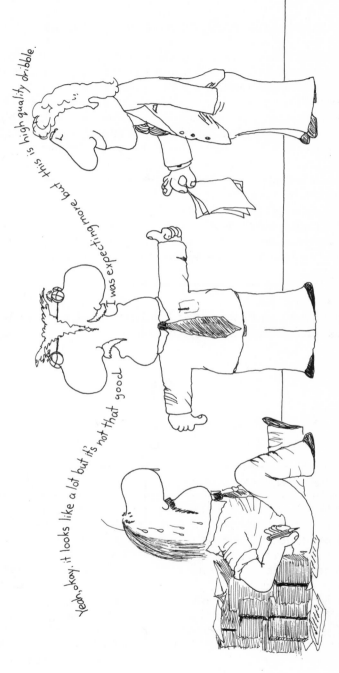

When quantity is missing, stress quality. When quality is missing, stress quantity. When both are missing, stress other criteria!

should be obvious that many rationales exist for justifying a positive recommendation when only an average amount of research or publication has been generated. The Agile Administrator would have a multitude of sophisticated rationales for justifying his positive recommendation based upon average performance in this criterion.

(4) *Faculty Member is Disliked* (A Negative Recommendation)
The Agile Administrator justifies his negative recommendation in the face of an average amount of publications by citing the fact that only a small amount of research (nothing to speak of) has been performed. That amount is not adequate for a positive recommendation. The A.A. will side-step any firm definition of "adequate," since this might come back to haunt him in later recommendations. Or, if forced to do so, the definition will be as ambiguous as that contained in the faculty manual, which is, in effect, no definition at all.

When quantity is missing (and "average" implies lack of quantity) then the Agile Administrator cites the lack of quantity as the basis for the negative recommendation. To be on safer grounds the Agile might even read the publication to get a personal assessment of the quality of the material, of course reaching the inescapable conclusion that quality is also missing. His recommendation will probably contain some oblique reference to the inordinate amount of time he personally spent in poring over the material to reach his negative assessment of quality.

If other aspects of the faculty member's performance or qualifications are *more* negative, then the Agile Administrator uses these items as the basis of the recommendation, and supports his conclusion with the negative assessment of research and publication. When one criterion looks negative it is easy to make the others look negative too. This "negative halo" effect is often used effectively (from his standpoint) by the Agile Administrator. Of course, a "positive halo" effect also exists and is used by the A.A.

Now we go to the final two situations regarding Absolute Data in the research/publications criterion, that is, when the faculty member has published what was determined to be an *above average* amount. The Law of Inverse Evaluation is just as appropriate in this situation as it has been for the other four conditions which we have discussed.

ABOVE AVERAGE RESEARCH /PUBLICATIONS (Exhibit 14)

(5) Faculty Member is Liked (A Positive Recommendation)
The Agile Administrator has the best of all worlds in making a pos-

itive recommendation in the face of such positive data. One of the more obvious signs of the true scholar is the quantity of scholarly output, namely, research and publications. This faculty member (who just happens to be in the favor of the A.A.) has clearly demonstrated that he is capable of making significant and substantial contributions to the literature of his or her field of expertise. A positive recommendation is certainly justified on the basis of such sound data. The quantity of such publications, not any assessment of their substance, is all that is needed by the Agile Administrator to accept the data as fully supporting the positive recommendations. Since each faculty member is presumed to be an expert in his own field, there is no need for the Agile to question the credibility of the publications in support of his recommendation. But quantity is a negative factor if the particular faculty member is not in the favor of the Agile and the research/publications record is above average. Here's how that works.

(6) Faculty Member is Disliked (A Negative Recommendation) Making a negative recommendation when the research/publications record seems to present a case for a positive recommendation requires a little more *intellectual flexibility* (a mild euphemism for academic dishonesty) than when the data seems to be consistent with the recommendation. However, it presents no real dilemma to the astute, facile Agile Administrator. In fact, some Agiles get a real kick out of justifying a recommendation when the data is at polar extremes. It gives them a chance to flex their intellectual muscles.

The A.A. justifies the negative recommendation on the basis that quality is obviously missing, implying that quality and quantity are mutually exclusive concepts. A proliferation of publications (proliferation sounds so negative) is tantamount to an admission of a lack of quality. "This faculty member is simply grinding out useless drivel that cannot by any stretch of the imagination be construed as a contribution to the literature."

If there happen to be several faculty members who are also active in research and publishing, the Agile might be able to undersell this faculty member's contribution by comparing it to others who have published more and better (according to the interpretation of the Agile). His stance is that there are more than enough researchers on the faculty, and this criteria is therefore taken as only one aspect of the overall evaluation of faculty members. This further illustrates the tactic of interpretating a criterion in which the faculty member is well qualified as an area that is not too critical on an overall basis—when the Agile wishes to make a recommendation that appears to be (or is) contrary to the data. On the other hand, if the faculty member

---

EXHIBIT 14.
The L.I.E. in Operation: Evaluation of an ABOVE AVERAGE Research/Publications Record

− −Negative Interpretation− −	+ +Positive Interpretation+ +
1. Quality is lacking, since quantity is evident.	1. Obvious sign of a scholar.
2. Not scholarly.	2. Scholarly work being produced.
3. Crass commercialism.	3. Written for the scholar, not for commercial exploitation.
4. Too practical, not academic.	4. Quality and quantity both evident.
5. Written for the practitioner, not the scholar.	5. Substantial contributions to the field.
6. Not in his/her area of expertise.	6. Above average productivity in this criterion.
7. Not a contribution to the field.	

---

is not well qualified and the Agile wishes to make a positive recommendation, the criterion is similarly interpreted as not too critical—*only one* of the four criteria upon which faculty members are evaluated.

If publications of the faculty member sell well, then this is viewed as *crass commercialism,* not academic scholarship. (*Crass commercialism* may only be a synonym for *academic jealousy.*) But if the publications do not sell well, then the material could hardly be of value if no one is buying it! This means that if the faculty member has above average publications and they sell well (or are widely cited), then a negative connotation of crass commercialism or academic journalism is evident. But if the publications are not widely cited or sold, then they lack merit. This is only one of the many neat traps which can be used effectively by the Agile Administrator as he weaves together his web of logic to support every recommendation based upon whatever data is presented to him.

But what if items are published which cannot be easily interpreted as lacking in scholarly content? How can the Agile Administrator properly interpret this situation? Quite easily! He defines the field of expertise of the faculty member so that the items do not make a significant and substantial contribution *to his or her area of speciality, as defined by the Agile.* Or the research/publications are defined so that they do not fit into the area of expertise of the faculty member. In effect, either the area of expertise or the nature of the publication is defined in such a manner that the two do not fit together, thus failing to meet the research/publication criterion as spelled out in the manual.

But what if the research/publications are scholarly (?), are a contribution (?), and are within the field of expertise (?) of the faculty member? Is the Agile Administrator stopped from making a negative recommendation in the face of such data? Certainly not! The Agile can always get seemingly positive data to support a negative interpretation. This is where real skill is needed and the true A.A. will rise to the occasion.[6]

Of course, the first approach is to try to ignore the data and to use other criteria that can more easily be interpreted to support the negative recommendation. Second, the word "significant" can be inserted in the evaluation process. Conceding that the research/publication is scholarly and does make a contribution, the A.A. will claim it fails to make a "significant" contribution as clearly stated in the faculty manual (and as interpreted by the A.A.). Of course the Agile may prefer not to address the issue of the rationale for the negative recommendation when the data appears to be very positive. Should he feel that the rationale might not be accepted as adequate support, there is always the tactical maneuver of claiming that the reason for the negative recommendation is detrimental to the best interests of the particular faculty member! It is potentially so damaging, it will not be in the immediate and long-term best interests to divulge it at this time (perhaps never.) This approach raises all kinds of possibilities for assuming very negative things about the

---

[6]It may appear that this book addresses negative recommendations far more often that positive ones. This is true because, when the Agile Administrator wants to make positive recommendation and the individual receives one, no problem is created. It is when negative recommendations are being made (despite the data) that grievance-laden situations emerge.

faculty member without having to state anything. (*"No manmade weapon has been devised that is so lethal, potent, or dangerous as words wrongly used."* – Larry Dorst.)

The Agile Administrator is able to hide the real reason for the negative recommendation (he dislikes the faculty member) under the guise of a personal concern for the faculty member. At the same time, serious doubts are raised in the minds of others about the faculty member. (The influence of innuendos can be far-reaching.)

I return to my previous contention! Whether the faculty member publishes nothing, a little, or a lot, the Agile will be able to find the rationale which supports any recommendation. *The only critical factor is whether the Agile Administrator likes the faculty member.*

And now, we will turn to *Trends* in research/publications, and how these can be used by the Agile Administrator to evaluate faculty members.

3.2   EVALUATING TREND DATA

"An author is a fool who, not content to having bored those who have lived with him, insists on boring future generations." – C. L. deMontesqueue

The uses and abuses of trend data (in general) was a subject that was discussed at length in Chapter 2, and will only be lightly touched upon in this section. The reader may wish to refer back to Exhibit 9 (page 37) to review the nine basic trend patterns. However, for purposes of simplicity, only three patterns will be used here: an UPWARD trend, a DOWNWARD trend, and a CONSTANT trend. No mention will be made about whether the trend line begins or ends above or below an average line, since the logic for interpretation is similar to that used in interpreting trend lines on teaching ratings. Instead, this section will present a brief overview of the Agile Administrator's interpretation of trends in research/publications (of course, using the L.I.E. and B.S.).

The use of trend data permits the A.A. to ignore, or minimize the impact of, *current* research/publications in reaching recommendations—positive or negative. In essence, a track record (trend) can (but need not) be injected into the faculty evaluation process and used in either manner, that is, to support a positive or negative recommendation.

Four situations may arise regarding a *track record* of publications and the presence or absence of *current* research/publications. These are indicated below, with a brief mention of how such conditions might be variously interpreted by the Agile Administrator.

(1) *The faculty member has a track record but no current publications.* If the Agile likes the faculty member then a positive recommendation is based upon the prior record of publications, and no mention is made of the lack of current publications. If the A.A. dislikes the faculty member, the negative recommendation is based upon a lack of current publications.

(2) *The faculty member has current publications but no track record.* A positive recommendation is based upon the presence of current publications, implying that a trend has been established that should continue into the foreseeable future. A negative recommendation is based upon the lack of an established record of publications, and current publications are interpreted to be out of character for this faculty member, while it is "too early to tell if a trend has been established."

(3) *The faculty member has both a track record and current publications.* If the A.A. likes the faculty member then both records are used as the basis of the positive recommendation. If the faculty member is disliked, then this criterion is considered to be of little value in an overall evaluation of the faculty member.

(4) *Of course, there might be NO track record and NO current publications.* If the faculty member is liked, then other criteria would be used to support the positive recommendation. If he is disliked, then the research/publication criterion is cited as the reason for the negative action that would inevitably follow.

Thus, whether one has established a pattern of research/publications and/or has current publications is meaningless. Only the interpretation of the situation by the A.A. has any meaning. (Does this suggest that personnel evaluation efforts have been misdirected into *developing* criteria when the effort should be directed towards *interpreting* criteria?)

The basis for the trend can either be ignored or assumed, whichever method best permits the A.A. to support the recommendation he wishes to make. For example, a downward trend in research/publications can be ascribed to a decline in research and publishing interest (negative) or be interpreted as simply a change in direction from articles to more substantial research (positive) requiring more time and spacing out the tangible results of one's efforts. Such polar interpretations show the true beauty of the Law of Inverse Evaluation, confirming the fact that the only meaningful aspect of the evaluation process is the relationship between the person being evaluated and the administrator making the evaluation. Let's see how

EXHIBIT 15.
The L.I.E. in Operation: Evaluation of an UPWARD TREND in Research/Publications

− −Negative Interpretation− −	+ +Positive Interpretation+ +
1. Might be a short-term aberration. 2. Must take a "wait-and-see" stance. 3. Trend is not prolonged or sustained enough to merit positive interpretation. 4. May be a sign of the future, but too early to tell. 5. Quality is missing. 6. Quantity is missing. 7. This is not a publish or perish environment. 8. This is a teaching unit.	1. Forerunner of many more contributions. 2. Trend is clearly set. 3. Future potential can and should be rewarded. 4. Quality is evident. 5. Quantity is evident. 6. Increasing productivity is shown in this criterion.

trend data on research and publications influence the situation (if at all), looking at three trend lines: UPWARD, DOWNWARD and CONSTANT.

*UPWARD TREND IN RESEARCH/PUBLICATIONS
(EXHIBIT 15)*

(a) POSITIVE Interpretation: This faculty member has clearly established a pattern of research and publications extending over a "considerable" period of time. The exact amount of time need not be stated, and what is "considerable" is open to subjective interpretation. There is every indication that the trend will continue upward; thus a positive recommendation for promotion, contract renewal or tenure is fully supported by the data.

(b) *NEGATIVE Interpretation:* The trend line is not prolonged or sustained enough to merit positive interpretation *at this point in time.* This may be a sign of contributions to the literature in the future (and we should certainly keep our eyes open to this possibility), but it is too early to tell—too premature to act. It would be better to take a wait-and-see posture. After all, this might be a short-term aberration. Besides, this is a teaching unit and research/publications represent only one of the four criteria.

DOWNWARD TREND IN RESEARCH /PUBLICATIONS (EXHIBIT 16)

(a) POSITIVE Interpretation: Such a trend line would not be prepared, since it appears to present data that is contrary to the recommendation. If there are recent publications, these would be cited and the trend ignored. Other factors such as teaching ratings would be positively interpreted and used as the basis of the positive recommendation. This faculty member may also have changed from short articles to long-term research efforts. Besides, not everyone is supposed to publish profusely. If research is in progress (doesn't every faculty member have at least one book that he is writing?), then this can be used to buttress the positive recommendation.

(b) *NEGATIVE Interpretation:* Here the trend line takes on significance, since on the surface it appears to support a negative recommendation. (A declining trend line implies something negative.) Obviously the research and publishing interest (and productivity) of this faculty member is slipping. It foreshadows a total lack of contribution to the literature in the future. The only course open to the Agile Administrator is to wait and see before making any positive recommendation (such as for promotion). But if the issue in question is tenure or contract renewal, then the Agile must make one of those hard decisions which face all administrators. He must "bite the bullet." Based upon the picture clearly presented by the declining trend line, he must make a negative recommendation in this most important criterion required by the faculty manual.

A CONSTANT TREND IN RESEARCH /PUBLICATIONS (EXHIBIT 17)

(a) POSITIVE Interpretation: There is a neutral connotation to a horizontal trend line, and therefore a positive recommendation

EXHIBIT 16.
The L.I.E. in Operation: Evaluation of a DOWNWARD TREND in Research/Publications

——Negative Interpretation——	++Positive Interpretation++
1. Research/publications effort is diminishing.	1. May be only a short-term aberration.
2. Foreshadows lack of contributions in the future.	2. (Cite absolute data if it presents a "better picture.")
3. Must take a "wait-and-see" attitude.	3. (Ignore the trend data.)
4. May present serious problems in the future.	4. (Highlight teaching ratings.)
5. This is a critical criterion.	5. Quality is improving, since quantity is being "intentionally reduced."
6. The trend is obviously negative.	6. Major effort being placed on long-term research efforts.
	7. This is not a publish or perish environment.
	8. Not everyone is expected to publish profusely.

based upon such a trend is relatively easy to support. If the *absolute data* (upon which the trend line was based) is all *above average,* then this point will be made by the A.A. in the recommendation. Should the absolute data all be *below average,* then the constant trend line will be used to support the positive recommendation. After all, there has been NO diminution of research/publications (as implied by a constant trend line). Steady progress has been noted; quality and quantity have been sustained; there *has* been output of research/publications. Moreover, if other aspects of the faculty member's performance or qualifications are more positive, then these will be used to support the positive recommendation.

(b) *NEGATIVE Interpretation:* A neutral interpretation can very easily be converted to a negative one by implying a lack of progress. If the absolute data is below average, then this data will be used and the constant trend line chart will not be prepared. Quantity will be cited by the Agile Administrator as being missing when the trend line is horizontal (although it should be intuitively obvious that a horizontal trend line could be based upon a very *high but steady* output of research/publications).

Certainly there has been no improvement in this criterion, and such lack of progress could be used as the basis of the recommendation. The strategically minded Agile will have cited this deficiency in a previous recommendation to lay the groundwork for this negative interpretation. In this case, *timing* of the previous recommendation is important. If the previous recommendation occurred late in

---

EXHIBIT 17.
The L.I.E. in Operation: Evaluation of a CONSTANT TREND in Research/Publications

− −Negative Interpretation− −	+ +Positive Interpretation+ +
1. No sign of progress in publications. 2. Quantity is not on the increase. 3. Progress is missing. 4. No improvement in research/publications record. 5. Quality is missing. 6. Quantity is missing.	1. Not a downward trend. 2. Constant publication record. 3. Quality is sustained. 4. Steady progress is evident. 5. No drop in quantity of research/publications.

the academic year, it may have been too late for the faculty member to correct the situation. Thus, the Agile Administrator is in an excellent position to cite his previous warning to the faculty member and base the negative recommendation upon no substantial progress.

3.3 SUMMARY STATEMENTS

1. When teaching effectiveness and research competence are both demanded, mediocrity is created in both, and excellence in neither.

2. The publish or perish syndrome is an anachronism of a prior time in academic history—one that should be seriously reviewed to see if it is still relevant today.

3. The Agile Administrator will not abandon the publication/research criterion since it is too useful a tool to him.

4. It is just as easy to justify a recommendation for tenure with no research/publications as it is to justify a terminal contract.

5. Agile Administrators overtly decry a publish or perish environment, yet covertly subscribe to such an environment, and enforce it, if appropriate.

6. Administrators who use "lack of publications" as justification for terminating faculty members are often the very same people who have never published anything remotely scholarly in their lives. Their personal lack of research/publications does not inhibit them in the least from expecting (and demanding) such performance from persons whom they evaluate.

7. The major purpose of academia—teaching—is still not recognized as an essential element in the faculty member's commitment. *Creating* knowledge (or giving the appearance of doing so), and not *imparting* knowledge, is the behavior pattern which is rewarded in academia.

8. To publish or perish, that is the (academic) question.

9. Research/publications are evaluated on many bases, but rarely on the content of the material.

10. Research/publications are expected to be (1) significant, (2) scholarly, (3) substantial, and (4) contributory . . . four terms upon which there is little if any agreement.

11. The scholarly rating of a publication is a direct function of the number of footnotes it contains.

12. When quantity is missing, quality is cited. When quality is missing, quantity is cited. When both are missing, then other criteria are used.

13. If absolute data cannot be readily interpreted to justify a positive or negative recommendation, then trend data will be used (and vice versa).

14. A downward trend has a negative connotation; an upward trend has a positive connotation; and a horizontal trend has a neutral connotation.

15. It seems that academia is doomed to continue living with one of the "prime voodoo fetishes of our times"—that everyone in academia must publish or leave academia.

16. If a faculty member writes a book that sells well, that is considered to be crass commercialism, hardly becoming a member of the academic community. On the other hand, should it not sell well, then it is considered to be of no value to anyone, or else they would buy it!

4 Professional Credentials

"Experience is the fool's best teacher. The wise do not need it."

— Welsh Proverb.

"An education is all that remains when we have forgotten all that we have been taught." — George Savile.

"Experience is the best teacher, but by the time you get through her school, life is over." — Anon.

"Knowledge is to know that you know nothing." — Anon.

"When you realize that you are not so wise today as you were yesterday, you are wiser today."

— Olin Miller.

"A learned man is an idler who kills time by study."

— George Bernard Shaw.

"A sheepskin is a helpful tool in earning a living which ranks next to shoeleather in importance." — Anon.

"Some administrators are educated beyond their intellect." — Anon.

4.0 PROFESSIONAL CREDENTIALS

"Intelligence appears to be the thing that enables a person to get along without education. Education appears to be the thing which enables a person to get along without intelligence." – Albert Edward Wigwam.

Professional credentials of faculty members can be classified as the possession of either: (a) appropriate terminal academic degrees, or (b) relevant and equivalent practical experience. Minimum requirements are generally established for each rank, and the administrator must evaluate each faculty member's credentials to determine if the credential criterion is being met. The question becomes: "What are the appropriate academic and non-academic credentials which will justify positive recommendations, and what deficiencies could (would) be cited as justifying negative recommendations?" The issue is one of a balance, or a trade-off, between academic preparation and practical experience. Ideally, one should be well-credentialed in both areas. This doesn't guarantee that you will meet this criterion, but it does make it easier for the A.A. to support you and slightly more difficult for him to oppose you.

EXHIBIT 18.
CRITERIA FOR EVALUATING FACULTY CREDENTIALS

Each faculty member who is hired or retained by the University should have the requisite background of academic and professional qualifications considered appropriate for the rank and position which he or she is expected to fill. The minimum acceptable level of credentials will include, but not be limited to, attaining the highest level of academic credentials considered appropriate for the field in which the faculty member will be teaching, and a satisfactory record of employment that is of sufficient duration and quality to satisfy the minimum requirements for the rank to which the faculty member is appointed or promoted. The University seeks to attract and retain a heterogeneous faculty balance in terms of academic qualifications and practial experience.

Exhibit 18 gives the general wording which might appear in a faculty manual, stipulating the minimum requirements to meet the credential criterion. This chapter discusses the ways in which the Agile Administrator uses this wording to support his recommendations.

This criterion is interpreted in an *un*usual manner: If you *have* terminal qualifications (a doctorate, a Ph.D., etc.), it will count nothing in your favor in the evaluation process. Should you *not* have this degree credential, it could be fatal to your academic career. This may appear to be contradictory (is the L.I.E. at work?) but is really easy to understand.

Not having the doctorate has been the stated reason for issuing terminal contracts to (firing) faculty members, but possession of a doctorate is seldom used as the basis for retaining someone on the faculty. Once you have the doctorate, then the other three criteria are used to evaluate your performance and credentials, and the doctorate is taken for granted ("After all, isn't this the minimum credential one should have to remain on the faculty?").

Thus we have the unusual situation in which a criterion is *meaningless when it is met,* and *critical when it is not met!* Not having a doctorate can kill your academic career, but having one may not keep it alive!

With this brief introduction, let's observe the Agile Administrator using the Basic Supposition and the Law of Inverse Evaluation in assessing credentials of faculty members. First, consider the Agile's assessment of *academic credentials.*

4.1   ACADEMIC CREDENTIALS

"The meaning of the Doctor of Philosophy Degree is that the recipient of instruction is examined for the last time in his life. After this, no new ideas can be imparted to him." – Stephen Leacock.

Meeting the academic credentials criterion is essentially a question of having the highest degree attainable in the field in which one teaches—usually a doctorate. It is difficult (but not impossible) for an Agile Administrator to claim that one does not have a doctorate when one, in fact, does have one. But the effect could be the same if the Agile chooses to achieve that objective through guile and cunning (more on this later). However, this criterion is generally not evaluated if you hold a doctorate, but is looked at very critically should you not have one, that is, fail to be "terminally qualified."[1]

Completion of a doctoral program should develop expertise in three areas:

1) Subject Matter (*What* is Taught)
2) Teaching Theory (*How* to Teach)
3) Learning Theory (*Who* is Taught)

Having a doctorate imples achievement of a high level of competence in the Subject Matter, and that implication is rarely questioned. (That is, it is rarely used as the basis for making a negative recommendation, since incompetence is difficult and time-consuming to prove.) Thus, if an Agile likes a faculty member who has a doctorate, then competence is not questioned, but is assumed by the mere possession of the doctorate. If the administrator dislikes the faculty member, other factors are interpreted to justify the almost inevitable negative recommendation.

Faculty members seldom receive education or training in teaching or learning theory.[2] In fact, in some doctoral programs, *potential faculty members* are *forbidden to teach* in those same programs which claim to be preparing them for teaching careers! It is assumed that having expertise in an area qualifies one to teach in it.[3] This assumption is made and also readily accepted as erroneous. *Admitting a mistake apparently relieves one of the necessity to correct it!*

Although the issue of competence may not be raised, other than through the use of student evaluations of teaching effectiveness, there is yet another way to interpet terminal qualifications of faculty members; that is the *relevance* of the degree.

The degree (education) of the faculty member should be *relevant* to the field in which he is teaching. The Agile Administrator who likes a faculty member has no difficulty relating any doctorate in any field to whatever the faculty member is teaching (since everything is

---

[1]This term generally refers to possession of a doctorate, but it is not so clear in such areas as Law, Accounting, and other areas where other methods of certification are used; for example, the CPA, CA, and LLB designations.

[2]I apologize to those institutions which include all three areas, and which, in effect, are seriously trying to prepare persons for teaching positions. Unfortunately, such doctoral programs are in the minority.

[3]Teaching ratings prepared by students represent an attempt to evaluate the ability to teach and knowledge of the subject matter. Methods for interpreting these findings were covered in Chapter 2, and are not re-introduced at this time.

related to everything else in some manner). Or the issue just would not be raised in an evaluation where the faculty member was liked and the degree was not completely relevant.[4]

If an Agile possesses any finesse at all, he is capable of interpreting the faculty member's area of interest in such a manner that either (1) the faculty member is not in possession of the *appropriate* terminal degree, or (2) the degree held is one that is *not* needed at the institution at this time, or in the near future. This means there is no guarantee that a person's doctorate will be interpreted as the one he needs to remain on the faculty—which in effect is like not having a doctorate at all. Now you see why I did not say it was impossible for an Agile to claim that a faculty member didn't have a doctorate when he did! The effect of such an interpretation is the same. (This interpretation of the doctorate is similar in concept to redefining a faculty member's expertise as a device for eliminating research/publications credits from his vita.)

Still another way to interpret academic degrees is by the *prestige rating* of the institution from which the degree was earned. Although all doctorates are doctorates, some are more equal than others. Whether a degree is from one of the top 10 schools or one of the bottom 10 may make a difference (*"A difference is a difference if it makes a difference."* – Anon.), although there would be a great deal of disagreement over which schools are in each of these categories. One could, probably, get some agreement on those schools which were "in the top" and those "near the bottom." Any further refinement in the classification would create arguments.

Ironically, I guess, the prestige rating of one's doctoral degree (really the institution which granted it) is based upon the CURRENT status of the institution, and has no bearing on the quality of the institution at the time that the degree was granted. This is an overall generalization, however, and like all generalizations, it is not entirely true. If a faculty member received a doctorate from Podunk U. 10 years ago when it was a flunky institution, and that institution has for some unknown reason risen to the status of one of the better schools, then the prestige of his degree has been enhanced in value. (Of

---

[4]This brings to mind the case of one faculty member who had three degrees in *biology* and taught courses in *business administration*. This professor had no difficulty getting promotions and tenure, since he was on the "favored list." It also brings to mind the strategy of some Agiles of getting faculty members to teach outside their field of expertise, anticipating low teaching ratings that could be used as the basis for negative recommendations. Unethical? I think so. Are you surprised? I think not.

course, the reverse is true, but not necessarily so. One quickly dissociates with an institution that has declined in prestige, and refers to the "good old days.")

Notice the additional degree of flexibility this gives the Agile Administrator in evaluating terminal academic qualifications of faculty members. This scenario emerges:

1. If the prestige has *risen* and the faculty member is liked, then the current rating of the school is used. If the faculty member is disliked, then the rating at the time the degree was earned is used in the evaulation.

2. If the prestige has *fallen,* and the faculty member is liked, then the time that the degree was granted is used to evaluate the doctorate. If the faculty member is disliked, then the current lower level of prestige is used to evaluate the doctorate.

3. If prestige has *remained the same* and is *high,* this fact is used for those faculty members who are liked, and ignored for those who are disliked. If it has *remained the same* and is *low,* this prestige rating is used to evaluate faculty members who are disliked, and ignored in the ratings of those who are liked.

Four other items regarding academic credentials should be briefly mentioned at this time: *honorary* doctorates, *degrees for sale, quasi*-doctorates, and the ABD.

An *honorary* doctorate is granted for any number of reasons—some very good, and others not so good. This is in contrast to an "earned" degree, one that is granted for the successful completion of an established doctoral program. The Agile Administrator is given some degree (no pun intended) of latitude (he would take it anyway) in interpreting honorary degrees and equating them with earned ones.

Degrees which have been *purchased* (some honorary degrees are bought too) are another matter.[5] These are not considered equivalent in any manner or form to earned or honorary degrees. Thus, the Agile may have to play it straight when interpreting purchased degrees. This might be one of the few cases in which a recommendation to hire, renew a contract, or otherwise take positive action would meet with outrage (if faculty are directly affected) when the recommendation is justified upon the basis of a degree that was bought. Of

---

[5]See *Degrees for Sale,* Lee Porter, Arco Publishing Co., Inc., New York, New York, 1972.

course, the A.A. would have no trouble making a negative recommendation when the justification stated that the faculty member did not have an earned degree.

There is a significant number of *quasi*-doctorates earned in foreign countries which have been peddled and accepted as bona fide doctorates, and used to secure tenure for their holders. If the holder of such a glorified degree is in the good graces of the Agile Administrator then no problem will be forthcoming. Should he fall from the graces of the Agile, then it is not too difficult to predict what kind of an evaluation would be forthcoming in the credentials criterion.

And, of course, there is always the *A*ll-*B*ut-*D*issertation (ABD) student/faculty member—one who has completed all requirements for the doctorate except the dissertation, or research project. Such a faculty member can usually remain on the faculty for a limited number of years in the ABD stage. When this time expires, the Agile has no difficulty recommending a terminal contract for (firing) the faculty member, but could, with the judicious use of the Law of Inverse Evaluation, make an exception and grant tenure or renew the contract. (One ABD summed it up this way: "I'm not worried whether I complete my doctoral program or not. If the dean likes me, I'll get tenure.")[6]

This returns us to the conclusion which we continue to reach: Credentials are meaningless in the evaluation process. In the hands of the Agile Administrator, there is an *avenue of interpretation* which leads directly to the foregone conclusion, either positive or negative.

And now, we follow the rationale of the Agile Administrator in evaluating non-academic credentials.

4.2   NON-ACADEMIC CREDENTIALS

"Experience teaches us that experience teaches us nothing." – André Maurois.

This section discusses the techniques by which the Agile Administrator tries to determine whether a faculty member has "relevant and appropriate experience" to compensate for, or supplement, academic credentials. This is an attempt to see if one's credentials

---

[6]This faculty member and the dean were of the same religious affiliation, in a unit in which this appeared to be the major relevant criterion for positive personnel actions. (The manual of course contained the standard non-discrimination clause.) This faculty member was aware of the Law of Inverse Evaluation, in principle if not by name.

give prima facie evidence of expertise, and whether the evidence supports a negative or a positive recommendation. (How foolish of me to phrase it this way, since I am sure that you are way ahead of me and know that whatever evidence is presented can be interpreted to support either point of view.)

Relevant experience usually refers to *practical* experience not, I repeat NOT, gained by attendance at formalized programs of instruction at academic institutions. (Is formalized instruction *im*practical?) For example, if one is to teach in the communications areas, and has been working with one or more of the "media," then this might be "proof" that he has attained a level of expertise similar to (but never the equivalent of) that which would be gained from completing an appropriate degree program at an academic institution.[7] Academic administrators would rarely admit that the *real* world might have produced someone with experience and expertise equivalent to an academic program. Admitting that some experience is "acceptable as a substitute" is another matter.

Exhibit 18 (page 70) describes the criterion for professional credentials, and contains the phrase "when appropriate." This small phrase of only two words gives the Agile Administrator wide latitude and discretion in deciding what is "practical, related experience." It permits the A.A. to assess the lack of a terminal academic degree and/or practical experience in any manner. Properly interpreting this phrase permits the Agile to hire a new faculty member, promote one, grant tenure, etc., upon the personal assessment of relative experience, or, similarly, to deny another person such positive actions simply by interpreting the criterion in an opposite fashion—stressing the essential need for appropriate terminal degrees.

How does this loophole affect faculty members who are already in the academic system? Obviously, the effect that it has is a direct and predictable function of the personal likes and dislikes of the Agile Administrator. If a faculty member is liked, then the A.A. can use the loophole to support positive recommendations of almost any kind by citing and interpreting experience in a favorable light for the person being evaluated. Such data can be used to support a weak case or to build a stronger case for a positive recommendation. On the

---

[7]Artists, writers, actors, government officials, etc., have attained some prominence (and one hopes a level of competence) which may qualify them to enter the ranks of academe (without degrees) after active and successful (?) careers. Many such persons do not have doctorates, but this presents no difficulty in evaluation of experience.

Not all degrees are earned!

other hand, should the Agile dislike the faculty member, then this clause either is ignored if it contains data which might reflect favorably on the faculty member, or is interpreted in a neutral or negative light, thus supporting a negative recommendation or disallowing a positive one. But what if the Agile Administrator wishes to hire someone who lacks the proper academic credentials but is obviously liked by the Agile? The clause "when appropriate," in effect, give the Agile a way to totally ignore all of the criteria *which current faculty members must meet* when he wishes to hire one of his cronies. A positive recommendation to hire an individual can be made based upon "equivalent" experience and qualifications. The implicit assumption is that, if a person is successful (whatever that means), then this success is a direct result of personal efforts and is evidence of having attained a level of expertise. Of course, such will be the case in some instances. But there is no *necessary* relationship between the position one attains and the degree of competence one has—particularly since there is no automatic assumption that having substantive knowledge immediately endows one with the temperament and ability to provide a stimulating and rewarding learning environment in academe. In fact, what makes one successful in one's field may be exactly what would make one a failure in the academic community, and vice versa.[8]

Seeing someone without the proper credentials hired (and usually at the higher ranks) is of no small concern to those faculty members who are expected to fully meet all criteria in the manual, and who have devoted their lives to the academic community. (A similar situation arises when an outsider is brought into any organization at a relatively high position.) The concern is particularly acute when faculty members are expected to wait 6 to 10 years to become a Full Professor, and someone from the outside is hired at that rank without having spent a single day in an academic institution. Yet these same faculty members may have full-time practical experience which is *totally ignored* in evaluating them for progression in the ranks. This is one of the more vivid illustrations of the L.I.E. in operation.

What if the *faculty* wishes to hire someone who does not have the right degrees, but who does possess an expertise the faculty thinks could be of benefit to the academic community? If the Agile Admin-

---

[8]A Professor and a Vice-President of a corporation were talking about changing careers; that is, the Vice-President going into academia, and the Professor going into the "real world." The Vice-President thought that having achieved V.P. status qualified him to be a Full Professor but was reluctant to admit that being a Full Professor qualified one to become a Vice-President.

istrator likes that person, then it is a relatively simple matter to use the "elastic clause" of the faculty manual to support an exception to the degree criterion.[9] Should he dislike the person, then he would become a stickler for the criterion and would make a case against the person. "After all, it would be grossly unfair to use one standard (require the doctorate) for our faculty, and yet ignore this criterion for someone from the outside." Using this strict interpretation (simply the L.I.E.) it is just as easy to present a case for hiring, or refusing to hire, a Nobel Prize winner.

And so we inexorably come to the inescapable conclusion that what is relevant and/or equivalent experience is simply a reflection of the personal likes and dislikes of the Agile Administrator. There appears to be no other meaningful way to define relevant experience.

This wide loophole in the method by which professional credentials are evaluated gives the Agile Administrator enormous potential for using or abusing the overall selection and evaluation process. When an administrator makes a recommendation which is based upon subjective judgment, it is very difficult to get another group (or higher level administrator) to superimpose a judgment over the initial recommendation.[10] Apparently this would wreak havoc in the academic community; so lower level judgments are often accepted even when higher level authorities have the power to counteract them, and even when such persons freely admit that the judgments appear to be incorrect. (*"When faced with two evils, select the lesser of the two."* – Anon.)

It is admittedly very difficult to define equivalent professional experience, and to equate actual experience with academic degree programs. These questions arise: What is professional competence? What is the trade-off between years of experience and completion of a degree program? What is the relationship between possession of knowledge and being able to effectively relate this in an academic setting?

Despite these obvious difficulties, there probably should be some way to permit the academic community to benefit from the services

---

[9]There is usually some stipulation in the manual, or one is simply understood, that permits the making of recommendations which are exceptions to the manual requirements. I have labeled this the "elastic clause."

[10]This reluctance to superimpose judgment is perhaps one of the reasons why grievance committees (discussed in more detail in Chapter 6) are ineffective. Such committees are equally reluctant to question the judgment of an administrator, even when they feel strongly that the judgment is incorrect.

of individuals who have achieved notable distinction in their fields of expertise, without the benefit (?) of the proper educational background (degrees). Perhaps what is needed is a more stringent control over this exception, controls far in excess of those which appear to be in existence at the present time. The stipulation may be acceptable, but the *interpretation* of it presents the problems. (Need I say it again? Data is meaningless. Only the personal likes and dislikes—whims—of the Agile Administrator have any meaning at all. The L.I.E. continues.)

4.3 SUMMARY STATEMENTS

1. Having the appropriate terminal degrees may prevent you from getting a terminal contract (a euphemism for being fired), but it may mean nothing in your favor in being evaluated.

2. Preparation for becoming a faculty member usually occurs in only one of the three areas in which preparation should reasonably be expected.

3. Many schools which have as their expressed purpose the training or education of teachers (professors) refuse to let such persons teach as part of their training and education.

4. Preparation for becoming a teacher often excludes coverage of learning and teaching theory.

5. An erroneous assumption prevalent in academia is that if one knows a subject well, he can teach it. This assumption is both made and at the same time accepted as incorrect.

6. Degrees are rarely evaluated on any qualitative basis. If one has a terminal degree, this is good; and if not, that is bad. The relative value of the substance of the degree is unimportant in the evaluation process.

7. The same relative weight is given to a doctorate earned 20 years ago, as is given to one earned this year.

8. Evaluation of a doctorate is normally based on the current prestige of the school from which it was earned, not on the reputation of the school at the time it was granted.

9. If a person has terminal qualifications these are taken for granted; the other three criteria are used to evaluate that person. Failing to have the terminal qualifications, however, may make this criterion the most important one.

10. Agile administrators can and do completely ignore the requirement for having terminal qualifications (a doctorate or equivalent) when they wish to hire someone they like, but impose that criteria rigidly when someone whom they do not like (and who may have superior and relevant experience) is recommended for hiring.

11. There is often little or no relationship between the subject matter studied in a doctoral degree program and the courses taught by that professor.

12. The equivalent experience loophole in the faculty manual gives the Agile Administrator enormous flexibility in hiring his cronies.

13. Faculty members who have dedicated their lives to academia are expected to fully meet (and be judged by) all criteria in the faculty manual, whereas friends of Agiles are often hired at the Full Professor level without meeting any of the criteria.

14. Relevant and equivalent experience is defined in any manner which the Agile Administrator wishes to use.

15. Relevant professional experience is often ignored in evaluating professors who are within the system, and is, conversely, often used as the sole basis for hiring persons who are otherwise completely unqualified for a faculty position.

5 Institutional Contributions

A Committee is:

> *. . . a group of people who keep minutes and lose hours!* – Anon.

> *. . . a group of people who take a long and torturous route to an obvious conclusion!* – Anon.

> *. . . a group of people who, individually, can do nothing, but collectively can meet and decide that nothing can be done!* – Anon.

> *. . . a group of people who have found a place to talk about something instead of doing anything.* – Anon.

> *. . . a cul-de-sac into which ideas are lured and then quietly strangled!* – J. A. Lincoln.

> *. . . successful when it has three members, one of whom happens to be absent and another **one** is sick!* – Hendrik W. Van Loon.

> *. . . usually organized for the purpose of delaying decision and hampering progress.* – Anon.

"In a committee, having a majority only means that all the fools are on one side." – Anon.

"A committee consisting of Agile Administrators is the greatest deliberative body in the world, but a group of bricklayers will run it a close second." – Anon.

"Having served on various committees, I have drawn up a list of rules:

> *Never arrive on time; this stamps you as a beginner.*
> *Don't say anything until the meeting is half over; this stamps you as wise.*
> *Be as vague as possible; this avoids irritating others.*
> *When in doubt, suggest a subcommittee be appointed.*
> *Be the first to move for adjournment; this will make you popular, since it's what everybody is waiting for."*
> – Harry Chapman

5.0 INSTITUTIONAL CONTRIBUTIONS

"Tradition has always dictated that it is far better to debate an important matter without settling it, than to settle it without debating it." – Anon.

In addition to being an effective teacher and researcher and being terminally qualified, each faculty member is obligated to the university and general community. This represents the fourth criterion in the faculty evaluation process. It is a catch-all category, inasmuch as it includes anything that cannot be subsumed under the other three criteria.

Each faculty member is considered a participant (member) of three communities: (1) the teaching unit which is his or her base of operations; (2) the university community of which that teaching unit is a part; and (3) the general community served by the institution (which with the larger universities is nationwide or worldwide in scope). Faculty members are expected to expend a certain portion of intellectual effort in each of these three communities. This expectation of performance is usually incorporated into the faculty manual under such titles as "Contribution to the University Community," "Professional Development," etc. Exhibit 19 gives the generalized

---

EXHIBIT 19.
CRITERIA FOR EVALUATING INSTITUTIONAL CONTRIBUTIONS

Each member of the faculty is expected to actively participate in, and contribute to, the general development of the particular teaching unit to which he is primarily responsible. Attendance and participation in faculty meetings and student/faculty functions will evidence such contribution. In addition, the skills and experience of the faculty member should be used in upgrading the broader institution of which his unit is a part. Attendance at Senate meetings and participation in University-wide committees would be evidence of such participation. The faculty should be concerned with, participate in, and contribute to the overall development of the society at large, which is being served by the university community. Public lectures, speeches, and participation in relevant and related professional organizations would be acceptable actions to fall within the purview of this criterion.

wording that might appear in a faculty manual to spell out this obligation to contribute to these three communities.

This criterion is slightly different from the other three. It is
more general in scope and includes activities outside the university
community. But it is similar, since it too provides a convenient method
for the A.A. to perpetuate his maneuvering in the evaluation process.

Within the university community, faculty members are expected
to serve on various committees (this subject will be discussed in more
detail later) and to take an active interest in the development and
problems of the university as a whole. Outside the university, faculty
members are expected to give speeches, attend professional meetings,
present papers at various functions, participate in local activities (such
as fund drives), do a reasonable amount of consulting (more on this
later), and become active members of the general community served
by the university.

To meet this contribution requirement, faculty members should
be on campus or at least available from the beginning of the academic
year in the fall until spring commencement. Office hours (6–9 per
week) are usually established and even maintained on occasion.[1] Once
spring graduation occurs, faculty members have the right to disap-
pear, and often do, suddenly emerging on campus just prior to or
during the first week of the fall semester.

Senior members of the faculty have perfected their spring disappearance to a high degree, whereas junior members make the mistake of being around and available during the summer. Somehow, if
you are around the Agile Administrator feels that you should be
available (without pay, of course) for student advising, special meetings, etc. If you do as he asks you might gain favor, and it might help
in later evaluating. Should you refuse to be taken advantage of, it will
surely do you no good. Perhaps absence *is* the best policy.

Perhaps this chapter should have been called "The Political Environment of Academia." To meet the criterion of institutional contributions, faculty members must participate in the political intrigues
of the system. Failure to participate (no matter how much you realize
that time is wasted) will quickly brand you as one who does not have
the interest of the institution at heart—one who is not willing to participate in its growth. However, should you make the mistake of really

---

[1]One student told me she had gone to her faculty advisor's office during
scheduled office hours at various times over a two-year period and had never
seen him. She finally left a note stating that she thought he did not exist. She
received no reply, so she may be right.

trying to facilitate its growth and solve some of its problems by suggesting changes, you will surely end up being scorned by those who know that only lip-service is really sought, not bona fide progress and growth. It is all right to *participate* in the activities of the university community and to give every outward appearance of wanting to make progress, but taking the flurry of activity too seriously may result in finding yourself on the short end of a terminal contract. *"Participation Without Performance"* is the covert motto of most organized activities and committees within the university community. *Vita-building* is another name for the same phenomenon.

I'm willing to admit that some activities and some committees actually do achieve something, but only after an inordinate amount of wasted time and effort, and after participants have given vent to their participation impulses. And those issues which were settled will reoccur within three years and be addressed as if they were entirely new problems, and another round of activities will commence. The author reviewed the minutes of faculty meetings of one institution for a 10-year period and was amazed (but shouldn't have been) at the minutia which was discussed. Issues kept cropping up as matters for faculty discussion in cycles of every three years. An issue would arise, be discussed for about a year before any action was taken, be forgotten for a year or two, and then arise seemingly as a new and vital issue, to be resolved within a year, and then forgotten, et cetera, ad nauseum. It almost seemed as if the faculty generated items for discussion to fill in the time that was scheduled for meetings, and as if no one ever remembered what motions were passed, what policies were adopted, and what decisions (if any) had been made.

Growth, progress, and change are disruptive of the status quo. This should serve as a warning to any well-intentioned faculty member who seriously thinks the bustle of activity in academia is heading in any positive direction. Being a disruptive force (unable to get along with one's peers) may be a legitimate justification for a faculty member's termination. Since growth, progress, and change may be interpreted as disruptive, faculty members would be well advised to give a wide berth to such situations at all times. (Consistent with the Law of Inverse Evaluation, the word "disruptive" can and does have many interpretations.) Avoidance of these situations may give some protection from an Agile Administrator who might brand progressive upstarts as disruptive elements which must be purged from the system.

This situation is a prime example of a case in which a faculty member may be fully qualified (exceeding the criteria in the manual) and still receive a terminal contract. Incidentally, the "disruptive factor clause" is seldom found in any published criteria, but would be assumed there if unleashed by Agile Administrators. Usually it is the subjective judgment of an administrator (or evaluation group) that makes the recommendation, and it would be very difficult for a faculty member to refute such a claim based upon a "subjective interpretation of the situation." (The courts have upheld terminations based upon "disruptive" charges. More on this later.)

Before discussing how faculty members are evaluated on their university/community contribution, it might be useful to briefly identify the two camps which appear to represent the extremes in university involvement (notice that the words *performance* and *contribution* were not used; *involvement* was). These two camps have been labeled Locals and Cosmopolitans, terms which have been used in the literature to rather broadly refer to the degree of involvement in university activities.[2]

LOCALS are those faculty members and administrators who are incessantly involved in committees at the teaching unit and university level. It seems that any committee being formed, even ad hoc committees, are fair game for the Locals, who run for almost every election and get appointed to almost every committee.

Within the university community they are known by everyone. Outside the university they are virtually unknown. (Locals are *big* in the small-time, but *small* in the big-time!) They seem to thrive on the academic environment, but avoid any outside activities. They enjoy the processes of academe and secondarily might even be interested in performing some useful functions. (Of course, sheer numbers of activities alone would mean that some results are achieved, and on occasion even significant results fortuitously emerge.) However, results are a by-product and not the purpose of Locals. Personal recognition and personal power are their real aims. Performance for the university is only a random fallout of voluminous activities.

COSMOPOLITANS, on the other hand, are primarily involved in activities *outside* the university community, with the local community, professional groups and associations, and the world at large. They have little time or interest in the mundane activities which consume a vast amount of time of the Locals. Cosmopolitans have a wider range of vision and a perspective that far exceeds the bounds of Locals. They think of national or global issues, whereas the Local is concerned with minutia by comparison. (But if you ask a Local if he is contributing to the university community he will be quick to assure

[2]For more details see: *Academic Gamesmanship,* Pierre van den Berghe, Abelard-Schuman, London, 1970, pp. 43–46.

you that his contributions are critical to the growth of the institution.) In fact, you would have some difficulty getting anyone to admit that he/she was a Local. The label has negative connotations. Some people (Cosmopolitans, no doubt) think that Locals are faculty members who tried to become Cosmopolitans and failed to make the grade.

By virtue of the fact that most of their time in the university community is spent on a multitude of committees, Locals gain enormous political power and, all too often, delight in exercising it over Cosmopolitans. This is particularly true when Locals serve on rank and tenure or other similarly titled committees, and Cosmopolitans are being considered for personnel actions. Some Locals (and Cosmopolitans for that matter) receive sheer pleasure from dissecting other faculty members on the operating tables of these teaching units and university committees, especially when the one being evaluated is more intellectually endowed than the one doing the evaluation. (The B.S. and L.I.E. move into full swing under such circumstances.)

This acquisition of political power by Locals helps explain why faculty members who are widely known in their fields (outside the university community) often have a great deal of difficulty in personnel actions (i.e., promotion, tenure, etc.). The Cosmopolitan has little time for, or interest in, playing the local political game and as a result is often at a disadvantage.

This presents a dilemma for the Cosmopolitan: how to spend enough time in the local community to protect himself from the adverse actions of Locals, without at the same time losing valuable contacts with his larger community of outside interests. The dilemma is usually resolved by spending time in local activities until tenure has been granted, then diminishing such activities (thus, turning their backs with little real risk of being hurt by the Locals). Salary increases and promotions might be slow, and below average, but these matters are not nearly as great a concern to the Cosmopolitans as they are to the Locals. Thus some sacrifice is needed by Cosmopolitans to permit them to pursue interests in their fields and still keep abreast of the local political scene. In the meantime, Locals continue to get on all committees and spend their time wallowing in the Local political scene, working on *in*significant projects which take significant amounts of time.[3] Since *the process is pleasing* to Locals, they participate to the hilt.

There are many instances, however, in which Cosmopolitans have a distinct advantage over Locals in sharing the rewards of the

---

[3]"A committee is a group of the unfit, appointed by the unwilling, to do the unnecessary." Henry Cooke.

university system. If their reputations are well established, they can threaten to quit, and use this as an effective means of getting their own way in the system.[4] Locals, on the other hand, are often treated with disrespect and scorn, and are not rewarded for long service to the university community. Thus, the prestige (or sources of funds) associated with Cosmopolitans often permits them to reap financial and other benefits of the local campus, since the university needs the Cosmopolitan; whereas the Local needs the university (and its political environment). Locals can and do create problems for Cosmopolitans (perhaps related to professional jealousies). (*"It has always been the occupation of the mediocre to harass the competent."* – Anon.) Cosmopolitans, however, have more clout, and usually end up getting their way—despite the use of the Basic Supposition and the Law of Inverse Evaluation by Locals to prevent such gains.[5]

And now, with this background of the atmosphere in which faculty members are supposed to make their contribution, let's continue our analysis of the Agile Administrator, using the B.S. and the L.I.E., as he/she evaluates university/community contribution.

5.1   WITHIN THE INSTITUTION

"A committee can be characterized as a group of people who think that nothing should be done for the first time." – Anon.

Each faculty member is expected to attend faculty meetings and to participate in the deliberations which are supposed to take place there. In addition, there are a multitude of committees on which everyone is expected to serve at one time or another.

First, we will explore how attendance at faculty meetings affects the contribution criterion, and then we will look at other committee activities.

---

[4]Cosmopolitans *can* threaten to quit since they are in demand at other institutions, often receive job offers, and earn more than Locals. Locals have very little desire for (or access to) mobility, and pay the price for this stability.
[5]Locals, being politically oriented, are extremely adept at the use of the B.S. and the L.I.E. Also, some Locals are Agile Administrators (as are some Cosmopolitans). It is not safe to assume that Agiles are either Locals or Cosmopolitans. They may be either, or both; or change from one posture to another as the situation dictates.

There is the mistaken belief that because faculty meetings take place so often (far too often for most members), faculties are always busy solving problems and making improvements in the institution. This is a common misconception, however, one not held by members of the academic community (who know better). Most faculty meetings are a complete waste of time, largely because faculty members and administrators (particularly Locals) are more concerned with the *appearance* of progress than the *actuality* of progress.

Many savor the political process. In fact, one of the status symbols for many Locals is the number of committees they are on at one time. An entire volume could be written on the futility of faculty meetings, and how they are perhaps the biggest time-wasters of all activities which take place in the institutional setting. Few constructive results ever result from faculty meetings, since most meetings address matters of little or no import. Should any member be so naïve as to suggest that the meeting address larger issues, to elevate the discussion to "goals" or more conceptual matters, such ideas are quickly dismissed as too broad or involved to handle at this time and needing more discussion (which either never takes place or, once begun, never ceases).

Faculty members like to deal with small problems which they can understand, even if these items are not the least bit important to the mission of the unit.

Larger issues, therefore, receive short shrift in faculty meetings, since there is very little incentive to address such matters. Perhaps that is why so many faculties lack direction. Establishing direction would involve a degree of cooperation among students, faculty, and administrators that is too difficult to achieve. Besides, the act of admitting that there is a lack of direction somehow seems to eliminate the need for further concern about the matter.

One quickly gets the idea that meeting the contribution criterion within the institution merely entails participating in meetings where little of substance is discussed, and nothing is accomplished. One who so thinks is essentially correct.

At this point, someone might wonder why faculty members attend such meetings at all. One reason was already mentioned: the desire to participate. Other reasons include the fact that such meetings are considered essential for meeting the contribution criterion, and such meetings are often called by administrators who like to bask in the reflected glory of their role as leaders of the meetings. Some administrators look for any excuse to call a meeting. In this way, these administrators can continue to reinforce their status position with the faculty.

Am I being unfair and overly critical of faculty members and the administrators who "run" such meetings? Anyone who has ever attended a faculty meeting will quickly confirm the counterproductive nature of such meetings. Thus, there is no reason to belabor the point here. However, despite admitted uselessness of such meetings, should a faculty member choose not to attend, he may find himself failing to meet the contribution criterion and suffering the wrath of the Agile Administrator. On the other hand, should he try to achieve anything at these meetings, he runs the risk of being labeled disruptive, naïve, liberal, or other similarly negative terms. The L.I.E. works in strange ways.

Non-attendance at faculty meetings or non-participation on committees invites a self-defeating interpretation or construction by the Agile Administrator. The only logical interpretation which the A.A. can make is an obvious lack of interest in the teaching unit and, indirectly, in the entire institution. (To paraphrase another well-known saying, "Participate or Perish.")

It is far more important (and infinitely more productive) to be *counted* in attendance than to actually attend faculty meetings.

This attendance requirement has some interesting side effects. Some faculty members have taken this attendance requirement literally, and usually attend faculty meetings until attendance is taken— then slip off to another "commitment." This gives the positive appearance of trying to attend faculty meetings even when one has a very busy schedule.

I recall one faculty member who used to bring galley proofs from his books to faculty meetings and work on them there. Every now and then he would stand up and make an intelligent statement (yes, it does happen) and then settle back down to his proofreading. This way he was able to kill two birds with one stone. Other "participants" read mail, prepared lectures, and otherwise tried to use the time productively.

Another ruse is to schedule office hours (or better still, a class) during the time period usually reserved for faculty meetings. Administrators who have caught on to this are setting aside times during the week in which no classes are offered and scheduling faculty meetings for such time periods. Faculty meetings must go on!

One enterprising faculty member arranged to schedule his office hours during the same time faculty meetings took place, and was also able to schedule one of his classes *for the same time*. I have no doubt that other faculty members have successfully pulled off this "triple coup." The game continues.

Keeping track of progress in the "committee route to tenure."

One wonders if such gyrations by faculty members to get maximum points towards the contribution criterion, with minimum time and effort, does not partially justify the Agile Administrator's use of the Basic Supposition and the Law of Inverse Evaluations in faculty evaluations.

Committee meetings can (yes, can) be useful to those who have chosen the *committee route to tenure*. Such persons can easily be identified by their seemingly total involvement with a number of committees in the teaching unit and the institution at large. They can also be identified by their lack of publications, research, or degree credentials.

Some of these faculty members take on administrative or quasi-administrative duties in the hopes that such involvement will gain them a positive recommendation for tenure and/or promotion. In some cases, faculty members are forced into administrative positions (no one else was available or would take the position). They perform the job well but may be denied tenure because the administrative task prevented them from publishing or completing their terminal degrees. Unfair? Yes; so what's new?

This is just another of the traps which exist in academia. Should the faculty member refuse the offer of an administrative position, he may lose favor with the administrator, with attendant consequences. On the other hand, to accept the position may result in not having sufficient time to prepare oneself in the other criteria areas. If you get the feeling that the evaluation process is a no-win situation, you are beginning to get an accurate assessment of the process.

Under the guise of making a massive commitment to the institution and dedicating themselves to its betterment, such persons are in reality taking what they hope (and pray) will be the shorter and easier route to permanence in academia—tenure.

When the actual tenure decision is reached, many who have taken the committee route are sadly disappointed. Although they are thanked profusely for the time they have devoted to the institution (and they may have made substantial improvements in educational matters), they are terminated for failing to meet some of the other established criteria, usually the terminal degree qualification or research/publications. However, should this faculty member be in the good graces of the administrator making the tenure recommendation, another scenario is not only possible, but highly likely. A rationale is developed that recommends tenure by making the contribution criterion more important than any or all of the other three. (As the L.I.E. would predict, meeting the contribution criterion may be the grounds for either termination or tenure, depending upon the personal likes and dislikes of the Agile.)

Other committees in which faculty members are expected to participate are those which supposedly have advisory input to the faculty evaluation process. Such committees may be titled: Promotion and Tenure Committee; Faculty Relations Committee; Rank and Tenure Committee, etc. These committees appear to be an effort on the part of the Agile Administrator to give the faculty and students a feeling that they are participating in decisions affecting them.

The Agile Administrator is a real diplomat at getting faculty and students to feel that they have participated in decision-making, by merely letting them "advise" him on matters. (*"Diplomacy is letting someone have YOUR way."* – Daniele Vare.) The faculty and students are content to discuss matters (become involved) and to delude themselves into thinking that they have had some substantive input into the evaluation process. Everyone goes away happy, especially the Agile Administrator.

In many ways, however, these committees often operate under the Basic Supposition and the Law of Inverse Evaluation, and exhibit the same behavior as the Agile Administrator. Perhaps a more descriptive name for such committees might be Agile Committees.[6]

Such committees often have members who delight in performing pseudo-evaluations of their peers, while trying to give the outward appearance of performing an objective evaluation. A case could probably be made that faculty members are more severe on their more qualified and competent peers than Agile Administrators ever dreamed of becoming. This is often the case with Locals who are jealous of more successful faculty members. With nothing but time on their hands, they preceed to get into all sorts of mischief.

Not only do these faculty committees operate under the Basic Supposition and use the Law of Inverse Evaluation, but there is the additional problem created by the action of group dynamics. For example, when a faculty member comes up for evaluation, if the first person takes a negative position the other members of the group might go off in that direction, and the faculty member has no chance of getting a fair evaluation. Moreover, in many cases few (if any) members of the committee even take the time to prepare themselves

---

[6]I apologize in advance for appearing to malign those committees of faculty members who take their job seriously and try to honestly and objectively evaluate their peers. I am sure that there must be such committees.

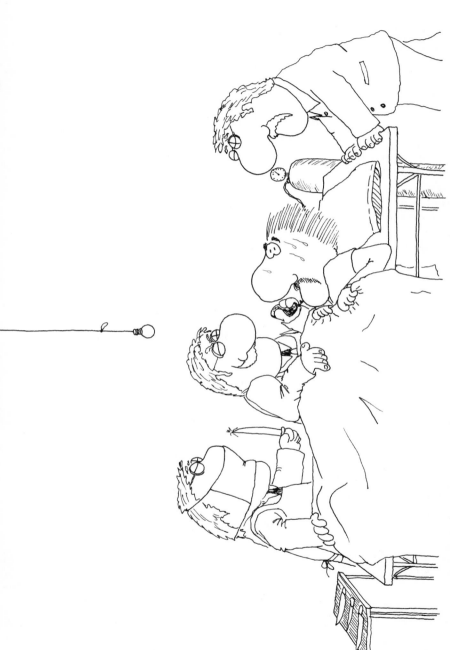

Performance Evaluation Committees delight in dissecting their more "richly endowed peers!"

for the evaluation by reading the material concerning the faculty member's performance or qualifications. After all, why should they? They already know which way they are going to vote (the B.S. at work).

In addition to faculty committee meetings, and committees to provide advice on the faculty evaluation process, there are innumerable other committees which may take up an inordinate amount of the faculty member's time throughout his career in academia. The degree of involvement and amount of committee activity can be fairly accurately predicted for the typical faculty member.

Exhibit 20 shows the pattern or trend of committee activity over the life span of the typical faculty member. There are certain predictable periods when this activity will peak. Specifically, there are three major periods of peak activity, and possibly two minor ones.

The *first major peak* in committee activity occurs when the faculty member initially joins the academic community. This peak is caused by one or more of three situations:

a.   The faculty member is young and naïve and is unable to avoid being placed on committees.
b.   The faculty member is being taken advantage of by senior members of the faculty, or by administrators.
c.   The faculty member is imbued with the desire to take positive action and to correct some of the obvious inadequacies of the academic system. It doesn't take long for him to recognize the futility of making substantial changes, and this reason for joining committees quickly subsides.

The *second major peak* occurs during the year just prior to the tenure decision, and the reason for this peak is patently clear—the hope of a favorable tenure decision.[7] At this point in time, assuming that this is the first time the faculty member is eligible for tenure, he is still under the delusion that the criteria specified in the faculty manual are objectively interpreted to make the recommendation. For some, it is a rude awakening to find out that this is not the case. This peak tapers off rather sharply about a year after tenure is granted (assuming it is). There isn't an immediate drop, since this would be too obvious. About a year lapses before the step-function-drop occurs. This one year lag is partially explained by (a) a desire to put on

---

[7]The far-sighted faculty member will arrange to be on the "tenure committee" at this point in time. After all, if you are going to put your future in somebody's hands, why not make them your own?

EXHIBIT 20.
**PEAKS IN COMMITTEE ACTIVITIES OF TYPICAL
FACULTY MEMBERS**

Note: This chart only shows the pattern of committee
involvement for the typical faculty member, not Locals or
Cosmopolitans. Locals would probably show a constant high
degree of involvement, indicating incessant activity in
committees. Cosmopolitans would show some involvement in
the pre-tenure years, then almost nothing until the year prior to
mandatory retirement, when there might be a slight rise in the
trend to stave off retirement. Locals might also increase their
activities just before retirement time.

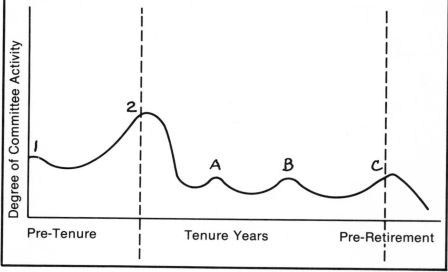

a good show during his first tenure year; (b) an attempt to justify the
drop in involvement that is imminent (being very involved one year
is certainly justification for reducing his load the following year);
(c) avoidance of criticism that "now that you got your tenure you are
no longer interested in the institution"; (d) proof that getting tenure
did not change his commitment to the institution, or (e) the simple
fact that he knows he cannot be fired (don't be too sure)[8] and wishes
to speak much more freely than he ever dared during the pre-tenure
years.

---

[8]"The only certainty is that nothing is certain." Pliny the Elder.

The Aging Agile serves as Honorary Chairman of the Ad Hoc Committee on the Abolition of Mandatory Retirement at Age 65.

The *third major peak* in committee activity occurs just prior to the mandatory retirement year. Here the faculty member may be trying to justify an extension of the contract beyond normal retirement age, or to prove to the institution and himself that his contribution to the institution is too valuable to be lost because of an arbitrary retirement policy. The more commitments one can assume just prior to retirement, the more ammunition one has to justify a continuation of employment.

There may be *two minor peaks* in committee activity occurring just prior to the time one is eligible for promotion (shown as points A and B on Exhibit 20). These may not occur if promotion and tenure are granted at the same time.

Notice that each of these peaks in activity is in no way related to any desire to make significant (there's that word again) changes or improvements in the institution, or to solve any particular problems. They are all related to a personal desire to present a favorable appearance for some positive personnel action (tenure, promotion, etc.).[9] The one small exception occurs when the new faculty member seriously thinks that committees are means for making changes and achieving progress. But this is such a fleeting exception, and is so quickly eliminated as a reason for participating in committees, that it can be conveniently ignored as part of the trend line. Vita-building is the major reason for committee participation, is a favorite pastime of the faculty, and is their attempt to make it difficult for the Agile Administrator to use the B.S. and L.I.E. against them. It is quite common to hear faculty members say that "the only reason for being on this committee is that it will look good on my vita." *Quantity* of items is sought (measured by number of lines) since both the Agile and the faculty know that measuring *quality* is difficult and is therefore seldom attempted. The appearance of activity is important. Actual achievements are nice, but seldom necessary.

Perhaps the faculty evaluation process forces vita-building. Since faculty manuals stipulate the criteria which will be used in the process, faculty members systematically collect as many items falling into these criteria areas as possible to build up their cases for positive personnel actions. An assessment of the vaule of such items is difficult, and it is easier to *assume their value* than to make any effort to *measure it.*

---

[9]I remember people at one organization staying late and calling their "boss" to ostensibly ask a question at a late hour, when, in reality, they were just letting him know that they were "working" late. Appearances *are* important.

How is this trend pattern, depicting an increase in committee activity just prior to tenure and promotion decision time, interpreted by the Agile Administrator? As you would guess; any way he wants to!

It can be disregarded as merely a flurry of activity designed to create the impression of performance, but not amounting to sufficient reason to merit a positive recommendation.

Conversely, it could be considered an indication of the faculty member's positive involvement in and commitment to the affairs of the institution, clearly meeting the contribution criterion.

But if the faculty member does not participate (does not show this predictable upsurge in activity prior to decision time), he runs the risk of failing to meet the contribution criterion (if he is disliked by the A.A.). However, failing to display the peak in activity (if one is liked) could be more than compensated for by the positive interpretation of the other three criteria areas. (After all, the contribution criterion is only one, not THE criterion.)

Again, whether the pattern of peaking committee activity is apparent or not is irrelevant to the recommendation. The Agile Administrator, and not the data, determines its relevance.

Committee activities have long been maligned (with good reason) in the literature as a useless vehicle in business, government, and the academic community. (*"To be honest, you must admit that committees make a constructive contribution to most institutions that amounts to exactly minus zero."* – Adapted from F. Scott Fitzgerald.)

Although this method for taking concerned action is misused in almost every organization, it is particularly mishandled in academia. Committees are used (a) as excuses to insure that no action takes place; (b) as indications of participation in the activities of the institution; (c) as means of giving the outward appearance of getting participation and consultation; (d) to impede progress; (e) to diffuse responsibility for action, and (f) to do *nothing* while giving the appearance of doing *something.*[10]

Committees are often formed on the spur of the moment (let's form a committee . . .) to handle a situation which arises, or for any of the purposes mentioned above, or others. Such ad hoc committees all too often become standing committees, remaining in existence (and fully staffed) long after the reason for creating the committee is forgotten.

---

[10]The "Do-Nothing" Committee has been used for some time. This is a group which meets to give the appearance that something is being done—when nothing of substance is under discussion. Galbraith covers this concept very well in *The Great Crash.*

This situation was beautifully illustrated at one institution when the Dean of the School requested nominations from the floor at a faculty meeting to fill positions on the Long Range Planning Committee (a standing committee). When a faculty member asked what the function of this committee was, *not one person* (including the Dean) knew exactly what the function of the committee was, nor why there ever was such a committee. (In all fairness to the Dean, it was his first semester in that position at that school.) Nonetheless, faculty members and students were duly nominated and elected to fill that committee—which never met once during the 2 ensuing academic years.

Perhaps it is time to abolish all committees in academia (including the Committee on Committees). Then only essential committees could be formed, and only on an ad hoc basis, terminating when the job of the committee was completed. This move would probably alleviate the situation for a short time. Eventually the same labyrinth of committees would come into existence, after which another purge could be effected, etc., and the cycle could be completed.

It is quite clear that such a move will not come about, since the committee structure serves the participation-without-performance desires of the Locals (and some Cosmopolitans). Committees are not joined for the purpose of achieving any objectives which may have been set (but which probably were *not* set) by the committee itself. Committees are joined for the purpose of vita-building or self-aggrandizement. Participation in committees, not performance on them, is somehow equated with contributing to the institution. This process of participation, while giving the illusion of performance, is sufficient to satisfy most faculty members, administrators and students.[11] And more importantly, in many cases it is sufficient to meet the contribution criterion.

There are, of course, other persons in academia (and outside the halls of academe) who attend committee meetings of various kinds to demonstrate their mastery of Robert's Rules of Order. They are far more concerned that parliamentary procedures be followed than with any substantive material that might (but probably won't) be discussed. Others see such meetings as opportunites to give vent to their latent Shakespearean leanings. (Agiles, faculty members, and students all suffer from this actor's malady.)

---

[11]"Patience is the most necessary qualification for academia; many a man would rather you heard his story than granted his request." The Earl of Chesterfield.

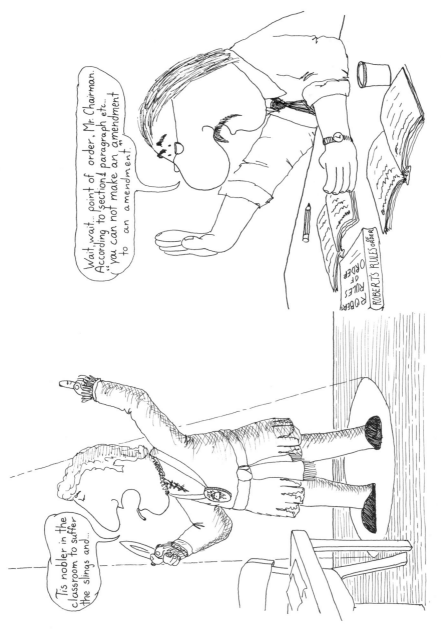

Committee Meetings provide opportunities to give vent to latent Shakespearean leanings, or to demonstrate one's vast knowledge about rules of Parliamentary Procedures.

5.2   OUTSIDE THE INSTITUTION

"To consult means to seek another's approval for a course already decided upon." – Ambrose Bierce.

In addition to taking an active part in committee work within the institution, each faculty member is supposed to participate in the larger community served by the institution. In some instances this might only be the community in which the institution is located; in other situations the community is nationwide; and in still others the global community is the frame of reference. When a faculty member goes on leave and joins a governmental agency, he is participating in the larger nationwide or global community, and may be considered as meeting the contribution criterion (subject to the interpretation of the Agile Administrator).

External participation can be evidenced by giving public lectures or speeches; presenting papers at relevant association meetings; conducting research (funded or not); consulting, etc. Each such activity may represent a line or lines on the curriculum vita, and records are kept to compile evidence of such activities for the annual faculty evaluation charade. Some faculty members keep "vita files," in which they sequester notes on all items which may be beneficial for the next round of discussions on salaries, promotion, tenure, etc. *Negative items never appear* in such files—only those items which may be worded or presented in a manner which reflects favorably on the faculty member in discussions with the administrator. Administrators, on the other hand, often keep separate files on faculty members, which contain only negative items to counteract the material presented by faculty members. *Positive items rarely appear* there, since the Agile Administrator can make a positive recommendation with little justification and with little risk that a faculty member will take offense.

Faculty members try to get maximum mileage for each external activity in which they engage. Thus, the ideal situation is to present at an association meeting a paper which is recognized by an honorium and which also counts as a publication (published in the proceedings). Money is made, a speech is counted, a publication is achieved, a meeting is attended, and the faculty member has gained further exposure for making more such external contributions. One such premium activity can represent several lines on the vita, indirectly suggesting a far greater involvement and contribution than might appear upon closer examination of the data. Administrators, however, are equally adept at *discounting* the activities of faculty members in order to moderate the apparent degree of involvement and contribution to the external community. The game continues!

Perhaps there is no more controversial area than *consulting*, which raises issues between the faculty member and the Agile Administrator and which is the bone of contention as to whether the faculty member is meeting the contribution criterion. Consulting (as you would surmise) can be interpreted as the reason for making a positive judgment that the faculty member is meeting the contribution criterion, or conversely, it can be used as the basis for termination for violating the full-time commitment to the institution.

This concept of full-time commitment is often stated or implied in the faculty manual, but its real meaning is seldom very clear to anyone. The general rule is one day for consulting per week. Let's look at both the positive and negative aspects of consulting, and how such activies on the part of faculty members might be evaluated by the Agile Administrator in determining whether the external contribution criterion has been met.[12]

On the *positive side,* consulting gives each faculty member an opportunity (should he choose to take it) to add to his personal level of expertise and background, while at the same time keeping abreast of what is happening out in the real world. (Many academics consider academia the real world, and the outside world as unreal. It is all a matter of perspective.) It is an opportunity to augment the meager incomes of professors (an image that's projected for obvious reasons). In many cases the faculty member can match or exceed his university salary by consulting fees.[13] Faculty members who are so esteemed by the outside world (that is, they make a lot of money) can be concluded to be highly qualified; having something to offer in their respective fields of expertise.

On the *negative side,* consulting may add nothing to the storehouse of knowledge of the faculty member as he engages in "dog and pony shows" in which the same drivel is spewed forth at lectures or speeches given to so many groups that the faculty member could

---

[12]At this point we will not discuss consulting as engaged in by the administrator, since administrators are not being evaluated in this book. One would expect that the performance of the Agile in consulting would *not* coincide with the expectations they hold for the faculty. (Another prime example of "don't do as I do, do as I say.")

[13]On the one hand, it may be easier for the female faculty member to match her academic salary by consulting because her salary is probably lower than her equally endowed and qualified male counterpart. On the other hand, it is more difficult because male consultants are hired more readily, and paid more than female consultants.

perform them almost unconsciously.[14] (How much does a professor learn by giving the same material to the same groups 50 different times? It is the old adage about 20 years experience or 1 year's experience 20 times.) Moreover, if the faculty member had no expertise or competence to begin with, giving such speeches or engaging in such consulting activities (should he have the good fortune to be hired) would not increase his knowledge any noticeable amount. Thus, being an active consultant may appear to be building one's credentials and knowledge but may in actuality be nothing of the sort. (Am I using the L.I.E.?)

To continue, the monetary implications of consulting present perhaps the biggest possible negative aspect of consulting. It is too easy to give in to the delicious temptation to make large sums of money (and take huge ego trips) and overextend oneself with so much consulting that one runs the risk of missing classes, office hours, and the other duties normally expected from faculty members—student advising, assistance in student research, etc. There is the distinct possibility that the faculty member will forget that his primary obligation should be to the institution which is paying his basic salary. (It is easy to see this situation arising when the university salary may only be enough to pay taxes on the consulting income.) Faculty members who forget their primary obligation to the institution are merely using the institution as a base of operations for their consulting.[15]

How does the Agile Administrator interpet the consulting activities of faculty members to determine if the contribution criterion is being met or violated? It comes as no surprise (I am sure) that whether one engages in consulting or not, or is successful or not, is irrelevant to the interpetation of the criterion. A plausible, logical rationale exists to relate any level of success at consulting to either a positive or negative recommendation. It goes this way: If a faculty member engages in consulting (and/or is successful at it), this may be

---

[14]One faculty member said he had given the same material to so many groups in so many locations that he felt like a robot. Once the proper button was pushed, he automatically gave the appropriate lecture with no conscious thoughts whatsoever.

[15]This dilemma between balancing the institutional obligation and the consulting practice was highlighted in an article by Roscow: "If the rising professor overextends himself in consulting, he is in trouble when tenure decision time comes. He has been a successful consultant at the expense of his academic commitments, but once he is out of a university environment, he becomes less attractive as a consultant."Should Professors Consult?," James P. Roscow, MBA, December 1974.

interpreted as an excessive amount of time and effort devoted outside the institution, or as a commercial desire to make money (ugh), or a clear violation of the one-day-per-week rule, thereby leaving the Agile Administrator no choice but to make a negative recommendation.

In fact, being successful at consulting can be and often is used to minimize the salary increase granted to such faculty members. One dean stated that it was fortunate that some of the faculty members were successful on the "outside," since this eased the budget strain considerably. The implication was clear: those who earned substantial amounts from consulting would receive smaller salary increases than their less successful peers. Here is a case of *success being punished,* and *failure being rewarded*—a frequent occurrence not only in academia but in other institutions as well.

On the other hand, such activities and successes at consulting can be positively interpreted as a clear indication that the faculty member has recognized competence (why else would companies pay for his services?). And since consulting is encouraged by the faculty manual under the contribution criterion, a positive recommendation (for tenure, promotion, etc.) is supported. This faculty member is meeting his obligation to become involved in, and contribute to, the external community being served by the institution.[16]

On the other hand, should no consulting be undertaken (or the faculty member not be successful at it), then this situation can be interpreted by the Agile as an indication that the faculty member lacks competence and is not contributing to the larger community served by the institution. The market has placed little (no?) value on his service. This may result in a negative recommendation. Conversely, the lack of consulting success or involvement may be interpreted as evidence that he is concentrating his activities and efforts on the *internal* institutional community, showing more than average dedication and commitment to the problems within the community, thus supporting a positive recommendation.

Thus, whether one engages in consulting or not, or is successful or not, need not (and will not) hinder the Agile Administrator from proceeding to the swift, sure completion of his recommendation.

---

[16]It does little harm (and might even do a little good), if one is successful at consulting, to include one's administrator in on the action. Sharing the wealth may be an excellent way to gain the favor of the administrator, which, it should be patently obvious at this point, is clearly the major relevant criterion in the evaluation process.

Whether one is active in the external community is irrelevant to the recommendation, if the A.A. chooses to make it irrelevant. The data does not interfere with the recommendation.

Whether the faculty member meets the contribution criterion is determined solely by the *attitude* of the Agile Administrator, and not by the *activities* of the faculty member. Such findings are, unfortunately, entirely consistent with the Basic Supposition and the Law of Inverse Evaluation.

5.3   SUMMARY STATEMENTS

1. Faculty members attend faculty meetings not because they are interested in what might be discussed, but because they don't want to be counted as absent.

2. It is far more important (and infinitely more productive) to be *counted* as being in attendance at a faculty meeting than to actually be in attendance.

3. "Vita-building" is one of the favorite pastimes of faculty members.

4. There are three major peaks in committee activity and two minor ones. The major ones occur (1) initially upon joining academia, (2) just prior to the tenure decision year, and (3) the year before mandatory retirement age. The minor ones occur just prior to being eligible for promotion.

5. None of the peaks in committee activity is related to any concern for the activities of the committees; all are self-interest oriented.

6. Most faculty meetings address minutia.

7. Participation on committees is considered synonomous with performance, although everyone knows better.

8. Committees are seldom joined for the purpose of assisting the committee to achieve any objectives, but more often for the purpose of vita-building or self-aggrandizement.

9. Many faculty members, students, and administrators see committee meetings as opportunities to give vent to their latent Shakespearean leanings, or to display their knowledge of Robert's Rules of Order.

10. Scheduling office hours, classes, and faculty meetings at the exact same time is the goal of many faculty members. Such a schedule maximizes minimum involvement.

11. Regarding university and teaching unit committees, the motto clearly is "participate or perish."

12. Senior faculty members have perfected their spring disappearance act to such an extent that even Houdini would be envious of their ability to perform it.

13. Agiles can be compared to chameleons in their ability to adjust to the data presented to them for evaluation.

14. Agile Administrators may be either Locals or Cosmopolitans.

15. Committees composed of faculty members who participate in the evaluation of faculty members use the Basic Supposition and the Law of Inverse Evaluation, perhaps to a greater degree than the Agile Administrator uses them.

16. Locals need the institution much more than it needs them.

17. Cosmopolitans can use the threat of quitting, since they have more opportunities for mobility than Locals.

18. Tenured faculty members often use the institution as a base of operations for their consulting activities.

19. Building a vita is the method used by faculty members to make it (more) difficult for the Agile Administrator to use the B.S. and L.I.E. against them. Sometimes it works.

6 Conclusions and Implications

"There are two kinds of administrators: those who think they are as good as anybody, and those who think they are better." — Anon.

"Inferior people have a way of making superior people feel inferior." — Adapted from Dudlye Field Malone.

"When all is said and done, a lot is said but very little is done." — Anon.

"Now that I have it all together I forgot where I put it." — Anon.

"The cause of inequity rests in the hearts and minds of men, and that is where improvement must take place." — Anon.

"Justice is a machine that, when someone just gives it a starting push, rolls on by itself." — Adapted from John Galsworth.

"So little done—so much to do." — Cecil John Rhode.

6.0   CONCLUSIONS AND IMPLICATIONS

"The Personnel Evaluation System is a carefully edged system of small lies and fake images." – Adapted from M. C. Goodall.

What can we conclude from our analysis of Agile Administrators, operating under the Basic Supposition and utilizing the Law of Inverse Evaluation? Is the personnel evaluation process simply a game of wits in which too many participants are unarmed? Are Agile Administrators, in reality, *unwitting incompetents*? (*"A person who does not know the truth about whether incompetence lies within himself, within others, or within the system."* – L. Peter.)

The first obvious conclusion is that there is no evaluation process—only a justification process. Data is not the source of recommendations, but is merely used to support recommendations which are arrived at before data is presented for evaluation. (*"A fact in itself is nothing. It is valuable only for what may be attached to it, or for the proof which it furnishes."* – Claude Bernard.)

Using the Law of Inverse Evaluation the Agile Administrator is able to develop the rationale to support a:

1. Positive recommendation with positive data.
2. Positive recommendation with negative data.
3. Negative recommendation with negative data.
4. Negative recommendation with positive data.

He is able to support such apparently diverse recommendations with rationales that are both plausible and logical enough to fool many people into accepting his actions. He does this by the methods indicated in Exhibit 21. And since there are four areas in which evaluation takes place, there will probably be both positive and negative data for any given faculty member. The Agile Administrator is able to use both types of data for both positive and negative recommendations. If the faculty member (employee) is liked, the negative data is ignored or misinterpreted and positive data is highlighted. If the faculty member (employee) is disliked, then positive data is ignored or misinterpreted and negative data is highlighted. The L.I.E. permits such gyrations. (*"The logic behind an Agile Administrator's recommendation is like quicksilver; if you try to put your thumb on it, you will find nothing under your thumb."* – Adapted from Austin O'Malley.)

(Mis)interpretation of the faculty manual is clearly no problem for the Agile. In fact, it is one of his favorite hobbies. The wording in faculty manuals, when they exist, is so vague and nebulous that Agiles can interpret it to justify any action based upon any data. The result is a justification (not an evaluation) process.

EXHIBIT 21.
SUMMARY OF METHODS FOR INTERPRETATION
OF DATA

If the person being evaluated is:	And the data is:	
	− −Negative− −	+ +Positive+ +
LIKED	Ignore or misinterpret.	and Highlight this data . . .
DISLIKED	Highlight this data . . .	and Ignore or Misinterpret

---

There are, however, three conclusions which stand out as particularly important lessons to be learned from our analysis of the faculty evaluation process:

1. *Competence has been redefined!* Faculty manuals try to define competence in terms of teaching, research, contributions to the community, and credentials. If competence implies receiving positive recommendations, then clearly the definition of competence which exists in academia is the ability to discover what Agile Administrators want, and cater to these personal idiosyncrasies. (Section 6.1 will elaborate on this disturbing conclusion.)

2. *Faculty grievances will continue to increase in number and intensity,* as a direct result of actions being taken by Agile Administrators! (Section 6.2 will discuss those grievance procedures which are designed to adjudicate disputes between faculty and administrators.)

3. *Getting your administrator to like you is the most important aspect of the faculty evaulation process!* Despite protestations to the contrary, and the existence of well-worded faculty manuals, the personal likes and dislikes of those making administrative recommendations are the only meaningful criteria in the evaluation process. (Section 6.3 will offer some hope and advice to those who would like to improve relations with their administrators.)

Let's begin by discussing the redefinition of competence.

6.1 REDEFINITION OF COMPETENCE

"Competence is defined as the ability to discover and cater to the superior's personal preferences." – L. Peter

The author of *The Peter Principle* and *The Peter Prescription* captured the essence of the redefinition of competence in the above quote. The Agile Administrator has personal likes and dislikes, and these personal preferences define competence, despite established criteria which might appear in organizational publications. Competence is subjectively interpreted as the ability to determine what the Agile Administrator likes and to cater to these whims.

Whether one is judged to be a competent researcher is *not* dependent upon the number or quality of books, monographs, or published research one generates, nor on the reputation of the journals in which one published. Competence is also *not* based upon the amount of funding one is able to secure for research projects. Whether one is competent enough to meet the research criterion is solely based upon the personal and subjective assessment of the Agile Administrator. And, according to the Basic Supposition, this will largely depend upon his personal predisposition towards the faculty member. Competence is determined in a similar manner in the areas of teaching, credentials, and contribution to the community. Results and performance do not produce competence; only the Agile's subjective interpretation or evaluation of these two factors produce it.

Is the faculty evaluation process a network of collegial interests wherein one must be a member of the "in group" in order to get the Basic Supposition and Law of Inverse Evaluation working for him? Or could the existence of Agile Administrators have jaded my view of the process, distorting it all out of proportion to reality? One conclusion does stand out as self-evident: there appears to be a reward system which favors those who are in the good graces of Agile Administrators (even if they are incompetent) and punishes those who are not (even if they are competent)! Mediocrity appears to be the norm of behavior which is being created and defended. There appears to be a conscious (or unconscious, if one wants to be kind) effort to drive those who are competent from the ranks of academia. (*"If you are competent then you can be sure that those who are less competent, or who do not like you, will view you as a target, and not as an object of admiration."* – Anon.)

This situation is almost as if Gresham's Law were at work in academia. In essence, this law states that "Bad money will drive good money out of circulation. When both are available, people will spend bad money and save the good money." In academia, the law might be rephrased: "Bad administrators drive good faculty members out of circulation." (Alas, perhaps I have indicted myself! I am a tenured faculty member and have *not* been driven from the system yet!)

The Basic Supposition and Law of Inverse Evaluation, in the hands of Agile Administrators, have created a system in which it may no longer be possible to encourage and reward competence. This seemingly ridiculous statement appears more plausible when one is aware of the *burden of competence* which has been recognized through the ages by some of the wisest men who have ever lived. (*"When you make your mark in the world, watch out for people with erasers."* – Anon. *"Woe unto you that all men speak well unto you."* – The Bible.)

Given the prima donna nature of the academic environment, and the *envy* which exists there (*"Envy is the adversary of the fortunate."* – Epictetus), perhaps some elaboration is required to support my contention that mediocrity is being fostered at the expense of competence.

Perhaps two extreme cases will illustrate this point. The first is a case in which a faculty member is *below average* (whatever that means) *in all four* criterion areas and the Agile Administrator *likes* him. The second extreme case is when a faculty member is *well above average in all four areas* and the Agile *dislikes* that faculty member. Can the Agile develop the logic to make a positive recommendation in case 1, and a negative recommendation in case 2?

When all criteria are below average, and the A.A. wishes to make a positive recommendation, he merely looks for the criterion that is most nearly average and uses that one to justify the recommendation. He would first look for various methods to present the data to make it appear in the most favorable light. And he would only use the data to support the recommendation if he were forced to submit some justification for it. Any Agile worthy of the name could concoct a rationale worded in such a fashion that at worst the faculty member would appear (to the unsuspecting public) to be average. Still, stretching the point a little, the Agile would look for any other positive attributes of the faculty member (hopefully something is positive, or can be interpreted as if it were positive) and use this as the rationale for the recommendation, alluding to the fact that the manual does not contain all criteria, but merely suggests four very broad areas. The A.A. could confidently rely upon the fact that few will challenge his subjective judgment (a term he would use, I am sure), and fewer still would probably analyze the data that was submitted with the recommendation. (*"All that is necessary for evil to triumph is that good men do nothing."* – Anon.)

The Agile Administrator therefore finds no difficulty in concocting a rationale to justify a positive recommendation to retain someone on the faculty who fails to meet *any one* of the four criteria. (Think how easy it would be if the faculty member only failed to meet one or two of the criterion areas!) The B.S. and L.I.E. can effectively be used to protect the incompetent. It can also be used to get rid of the competent, that is, someone who is far above average, even excellent, in *all four* criterion areas.

This second extreme case, while seeming to be a difficult one to interpret in an opposite (negative) manner, is in reality very easily interpreted to justify a negative recommendation. In fact, *three* very plausible and logical routes are available, and all are consistent with the B.S. and the L.I.E.

(1) First the Agile would probably admit that the faculty member is at least average in the criterion areas. This has two benefits: first, admitting to something positive lends an air of objectivity and fairness to the recommendation; second, it understates the case by the use of the phrase "at least average," when in reality the credentials are far above average. Then the Agile concludes, based upon his subjective judgment, that the faculty member is only performing well in the areas for *his or her own self-interest* (self-aggrandizement may be a more pretentious term), and not for the benefit of the institution or unit in which he or she is located. Ascribing self-serving, selfish motives to the faculty member allows the data to appear on paper to be positive, but the interpretation to be negative. In effect, the Agile Administrator has neatly substituted one nebulous criterion for the four established ones, and this is a criterion which is not susceptible to disproof since it deals with imputed motives. Besides, with the degree of personal and professional jealousy which exists in academia and elsewhere—and the predisposition to believe the worst about the best—the more competent the faculty member, the more apt the Agile is to be successful in this polar interpretation. (*"A genius is a person that dunces are all in confederacy against."* – Adapted from Jonathan Swift.)

Here we have the supreme test of the Basic Supposition and the Law of Inverse Evaluation, and both pass (fail?) with flying colors. All the data is highly favorable but a logical rationale exists to support

My teaching ratings are the best in the unit; I have served on several important committees; I have a doctorate and I have over twenty publications. Do you think these qualifications will be enough for me to get tenure?
Yes;... if the dean likes you.

an unfavorable recommendation.[1] In fact, two additional rationales are available for the A.A. to reject competence (which implies retention of mediocrity). (*"To be content with mediocrity is a tragedy."* – Ruth Smeltzer.)

(2) The second logical path to a negative recommendation when all four criterion areas are well above average is to label the faculty member a "disruptive force." This is an effort to weakly admit that the faculty member appears on paper to meet the criteria for a positive action. Then the contribution criterion is expanded to include the ability to get along with one's peers (which really means getting along with the Agile). Being a disruptive force has a very negative connotation, and when the term is used to justify a negative recommendation it is little wonder that a negative interpretation is reached. But it is well to remember that any term can be interpreted in polar extremes (the L.I.E.), and "disruptive" can be *very positive* as well as *very negative.*

Competence in the midst of mediocrity would certainly be disruptive, and so would the presence of those who were seeking progress and change in an atmosphere in which the majority (those in power) merely aspire to maintenance of the status quo. (*"If you insist upon standing still, stand aside; for others may be going someplace."* – Anon.) Thus, being competent can be considered disruptive just as easily as being militant and hostile can be.

(3) The third way to support a negative recommendation when all data is positive is slightly more devious, and definitely more *un*fair. (So, who said anything about being fair?) Should all else fail, the Agile can substantiate a negative recommendation by alluding to the fact that the true reasons for the negative recommendation are so potentially damaging to the faculty member that they cannot be divulged. (*"Rumors are the favorite weapons of the assassins of character."* – Ambrose Bierce.) Here the Agile puts himself in the position of protector of the faculty member, when he is in fact possibly destroying him. (This approach even seems admirable—that the Agile would refuse to injure the faculty member.) Thus, the Agile is able to submit a rationale which says nothing, creates a negative aura around the faculty member, gives no firm basis for a grievance, arouses the sadistic suspicions

---

[1]Before you accuse me of taking leave of my senses, or exaggerating for effect, let me assure you that there are instances in which this identical situation has arisen, and doubtless more cases will arise in the future unless all Agile Administrators are routed out of the system, an unlikely prospect considering the magnitude of the task.

of all who are aware of the act,[2] and all the while portrays the Agile as a defender of the faculty member. (This use of the B.S. and L.I.E. is scary, when its full implications sink in!)

Let's digress for a moment to a topic that is near and dear to everyone, particularly in academia: compensation. The issue of salaries has been intentionally skirted throughout the book. But salary should be one of the key components of every evaluation process. There should be a direct and positive relationship between credentials and performance and the salary one receives. Unfortunately, any correlation which exists is probably a random occurrence rather than the result of a deliberate planning. In fact, one could probably make a strong case (using the L.I.E.) for the existence of an *inverse* correlation between performance and salary received. At one institution the Dean rated one faculty member as the lowest performer on the faculty, one he wished he could terminate. He rated another as one of the top three performers in the department. Yet both individuals received identical salary increases!

The *salary* of a faculty member can be classified as *below average, average,* or *above average* by the judicious use of the L.I.E., and by selecting the appropriate standard to compare the salary against. For example, a salary might be *below* the average for the rank in the department, *above* the average for the rank in the university, and *equal* to the average for the rank in the American Association of University Professors guidelines. *Selecting the standard classifies the salary!* This is just another indication of the flexibility the Agile Administrator has (and uses) in interpreting salaries to determine who shall get how much at salary review time.

The L.I.E. provides adequate rationale to give an increase of any size to any faculty member and appear to be completely justified. It goes something like this: If the faculty member is liked, then the current salary could be interpreted as not commensurate with the performance as evaluated by the Agile, thus justifying a larger than average salary increase. If the faculty member is disliked, then the current salary is interpreted as already above average, thus necessitating a smaller than average increase to keep his salary in line. What kind of logic is this? (*To answer my own question: "Logic is neither a science nor an act, but a dodge."* – Benjamin Jowett.)

Not only can the L.I.E. provide a basis for classifying salaries relative to some average (and to justify salary increases of any size),

---

[2]'Do not fear your motives being misunderstood, or not understood at all. Fear more for them to be understood in their entirety.' Franz Marchault.

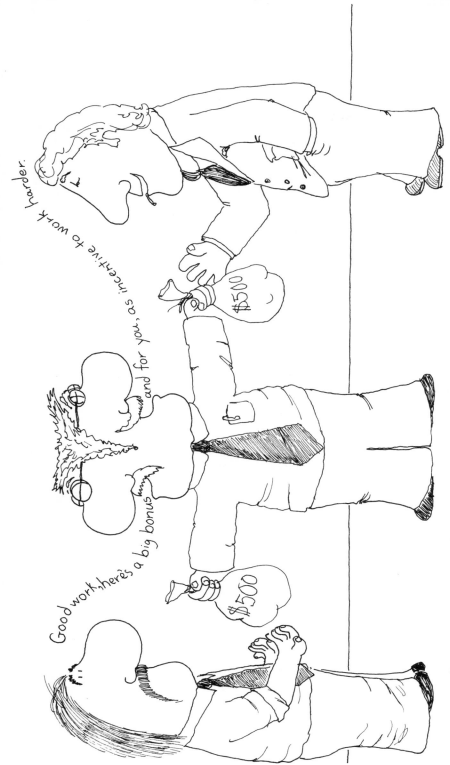

One wonders if there is an inverse relationship between performance and rewards!

but it also permits polar interpretations of salaries which have thereby been classified as above or below average. Average salaries can also be interpreted in this polar fashion.

An *above average* salary can be interpreted positively as an indication that the faculty member is better than average in performance and is being rewarded accordingly. Or it could be interpreted negatively to be an indication that the salary is more than one deserves. Interpreted in a positive manner, it permits the granting of a higher than average increase, and in the negative manner it permits granting of an average or smaller than average increase. (Keep in mind that the standard which determines whether a salary is above or below average was probably selected by the Agile Administrator, and that act classified the salary.)

A *below average* salary can be interpreted positively as an indication that the faculty member is not being paid commensurate with his or her performance, thus justifying a larger than average increase. On the other hand, it could be interpreted negatively as *de facto evidence* of below average performance and meriting a below average salary increase. Here we have the ironic case of a low salary being used to justify a low salary! And, as previously stated, a high salary was used as the basis for justifying a smaller than average increase!

Additionally, it could be stated that *someone* has to be below average. This occurs when a faculty member complains that he or she is being paid below the average of ??? (whatever would permit the faculty member to classify his or her salary as being below it).

Thus, salary negotiations are susceptible to the Basic Supposition and the Law of Inverse Evaluation. There are more than enough rationales to permit the Agile Administrator to (1) classify a salary as above, below, or average, and (2) interpret that classification of salary in a manner that would support an increase of any size. And if such options exist, you can be sure that Agile Administrators know about and use them to reward either competence or mediocrity.

Perhaps the real source of the problem in competence being redefined lies not with Agile Administrators, but with those who are responsible for Agiles becoming administrators! For if Agiles were not in administrative positions, they would not be sitting in judgment of others.

The lack of administrative talent—real talent—is very easy to understand. Those faculty members who are most competent in administration rarely seek or accept administrative positions. On the other hand, faculty members who are least qualified for such positions actively seek them—not because they want to perform the task, but because they want the position.[3] Ironically, these lesser qualified persons usually get selected, because faculty members are not prone to select administrators who are competent—that presents a serious threat to the status quo and might disrupt the autonomy enjoyed by those who have a weak and ineffective administrator. (*"He who is firmly seated in authority soon learns to think of security and not of progress."* – Adapted from James Russell Lowell.) Thus, before we place the entire burden of guilt on current administrators, we must first chastize those who selected them for the positions. People prefer an administrator who is safe over one who is brilliant.

This situation illustrates another contradiction in academia: to be well qualified for a position almost assures that you will *not* be selected for it, and to be poorly qualified almost assures your selection to the position. Thus we continue to perpetuate an atmosphere within which mediocrity can and will flourish, and competence will be discouraged. (*"Every kind of discrimination is a protection of the incompetent against the competent with the result that the motive to become competent is taken away."* – Lowes Dickenson Goldsworthy.) One can only wonder how long society will condone evaluation systems which retain and reward mediocrity while discouraging and punishing competence.

In view of this redefinition of competence, we can expect that those who are truly competent will not take such abuse lying down; more of them will resort to the grievance machinery. Let's see how that process works.

6.2   THE GRIEVANCE PROCESS

"I know that I am among civilized men because they are fighting so savagely." – Voltaire.

One of the more obvious implications of Agile Administrators operating under the Basic Supposition and using the Law of Inverse Evaluation is a noticeable rise in the incidences of grievances being filed. It is little wonder, in view of what has been discussed so far, that we have seen (and should continue to see) aggrieved individuals, armed with their lawyers, heading for the grievance process. With

---

[3]"Many people who covet positions of authority have no desire for the accompanying responsibility." Anon. Perhaps the best candidates for administrative positions are those who want to *do* the job, not those who *want* the position!

such flagrant abuses of the evaluation system well entrenched, and with few positive signs of any purging of Agile Administrators or of the system, it is logical to expect that personal dissatisfaction will be reflected in formal grievances. In fact, some grievances are intentionally created by a few (too many) Agile Administrators.

Some administrators take great pride in becoming the "leading grievance creator" on campus. Perhaps there is one administrator in each institution who lays claim to the title! Such administrators feel that each grievance filed is another notch in their title, and they seem to find delight in the misfortunes and miseries of others. (*"Never find delight in another man's misfortune."* – Syrus.) They have no concern for the anguish which the grievance process creates, and often are unconcerned as to whether the faculty member is successful with the grievance or not. They proudly tell the "corporation council" that the matter does not concern them (the Agiles); that it is the job of the counselor to handle all grievances. After all, isn't that what these internal lawyers are getting paid for: to represent the administration in skirmishes with the faculty over personnel actions? Thus, any assumption that administrators wish to avoid grievances would not apply to some administrators. We can assume that grievances will be with us for some time, even if major reforms are implemented in the evaluation process.

What happens when a faculty member feels aggrieved? If the faculty member has been treated in a manner which he feels is inconsistent with his record of performance and qualifications, then he must decide whether he will accept the recommendation and slip quietly into academic oblivion, or fight the system and the recommendation. Should he choose to accept the recommendation (and leave, in cases of termination or non-renewal of contract), then it will be assumed that the recommendation is merited, that the faculty member lacks gumption to fight for his rights, that he is politically inept, or other similarly derogatory terms . . . all proving that the original recommendation of the administrator was justified after all. Should he choose to stay and fight and to file the grievance, then he will be branded as a troublemaker who won't go away; one who wants to fight city hall or fails to accept the inevitable. Notice that whether one chooses to fight or to give in, he may be cast in a negative light, and probably will be. In academia (and elsewhere I am sure) being accused of anything is prima facie evidence that the situation does, in fact, exist. This makes it extremely difficult for the faculty member to defend himself, since he is starting an uphill battle. (*"That man is wicked! When he is attacked, he defends himself."* – Anon.) As previously stated, people are just too willing, eager, and ready to believe the

The Grievance Machinery may be more apparent than real, and may have huge doses of the Basic Supposition and the Law of Inverse Evaluation.

worst, even about the best (who are often put in positions of having to fight to remain on the faculty).[4]

However, should the faculty member decide to file a formal grievance, timing must be considered. If the grievance is filed too quickly then the implicit assumption is that he did not give the informal process sufficient time to work, and he may have to go back to try the informal system, which will probably be useless anyway. Should the faculty member be too slow in filing the grievance, he runs the risk of the grievance committee concluding that the statute of limitations has expired. ("If you thought you had a grievance, why didn't you come to us then? It's too late now for us to do anything about the matter!") Thus the dichotomy exists relative to timing of the grievance. "Look before you leap" and "He who hesitates is lost" are both appropriate methods for describing this timing situation. (*"Almost every wise saying has an opposite one, no less wise, to balance it."* – George Santayana.) The L.I.E. works in strange ways.

Once the grievance machinery has been set in motion, several things will immediately happen to the faculty member. He will, of course, be presumed guilty until proven innocent. A cloud of doubt will hang heavy over him. Other faculty members may avoid him, lest they be classed as of the same ilk and guilty by association.[5]

A campaign of rumor, gossip, and slander may be initiated against him. (*"Some people will believe anything if it is whispered to them."* – Anon.) He will be advised by many to simply go away (a tempting escape). In short, he will become a totally negative individual, much like a leper, to be avoided and pitied! Even his friends (should they still admit that they *are* his friends, rather than take a neutral posture) may be subjected to less than satisfactory treatment from the Agile

---

[4]In fact, at some institutions, becoming a good teacher, researcher, contributor, etc. is tantamount to asking for a recommendation that is grievable. It seems that the best teachers are often being issued terminal contracts, not being granted tenure, or being denied promotions. Competence is still one of the heavy burdens one must carry if one is in the midst of mediocrity and/or incompetence. There may be one saving grace to this situation (however small): "The injustice to an individual is sometimes of service to the public. Facts are apt to alarm us more than the most dangerous principles." Anon.

[5]At one institution, when a faculty member filed a grievance, other faculty members would check down the hall before entering his office, lest they be seen cavorting with the aggrieved party and suffer the wrath of the Agile Administrator.

Administrator. (*"Justice will be achieved only when those who are not injured feel as indignant as those who are."* – Anon.)

Once the grievance has been filed, there is usually a mechanism within the institution—a Grievance Committee—supposedly for handling it. In some cases an ad hoc committee is created to handle the situation. This may be such a time-consuming process that the faculty member gives up in disgust, and the issue is settled. (Perhaps the minimum time one should expect for a grievance to run its course is one year). The procedures for operation of the grievance committee either are spelled out in the faculty manual or are established on a case-by-case basis. The process generally follows this pattern with perhaps many variations.

1. An administrative action is taken for which the faculty member feels aggrieved. He/she tries for an *informal* settlement of the matter, within the smallest unit of the institution, and among only the direct parties of the grievance issue. If this fails, then the *formal* process is begun.
2. A formal grievance, usually in writing, is filed with the Grievance Committee.
3. The Grievance Committee tries for an informal settlement. If this fails, and the committee feels that the grievance has merit, then a formal hearing may take place.
4. After gathering all data and having the parties to the grievance present their respective sides, the committee prepares a recommendation. (They seldom have anything other than *advisory* authority to an administrator within the institution.)
5. The Administrator makes a decision on the matter, either (1) upholding the original administrative action, (2) finding in favor of the aggrieved faculty member, or (3) suggesting other methods for resolving the matter.

It would appear, on the surface, that the faculty member has been provided with a process which will permit him to secure justice from arbitrary actions of administrators. (*"Justice is truth in action."* – Joseph Joubert.) In reality, the process may be less than meaningless. Let's continue the scenario.

This committee may act as the embodiment of an Agile Administrator, or may seriously attempt to resolve the grievance situation. Its work generally revolves around making a decision as to whether there has been: (1) a violation of *procedural due process*—the procedures used to reach the negative recommendation (who would file a grievance against a positive recommendation?) were not followed, or

(2) a violation of *substantive due process*—the data upon which the re-commendation was based appears to be inconsistent with the recom-mendation, or (3) violation in both areas.

Should the committee decide (the B.S. at work) that there will be no basis for a grievance, they can take the following action:

> If the grievance was based upon procedural due process (as interpreted by the grievance committee), then the com-mittee dismisses the grievance by stating that it does not have jurisdiction over procedural matters. Instead, it only deals with the substance of faculty evaluation recommen-dations. If, however, the grievance was based upon sub-stantive due process (as interpreted by the grievance com-mittee), then the committee dismisses the grievance on the basis that it considers its scope to be limited to violations of procedural due process. (After all, the grievance com-mittee can't superimpose its judgment over the judgment of those persons closest to the particular faculty member.) If the grievance happens to be based upon an alleged vi-olation of *both* procedural and substantive due process, then the committee could state that no clearcut grounds for a grievance have been established and it is unable to act upon the grievance. (An alert faculty member might avoid this jurisdictional problem by getting the Grievance Committee to specify its jurisdiction before the grievance is filed.)

However, should members of the committee decide that there is a valid basis for a grievance (the B.S. at work again?), or should they dislike the administrator, like the faculty member, or both, or just want to justify their existence, then they might taken this course:

> The committee can conclude that the faculty member has presented a bona fide case for a grievance, and can rec-ommend a reversal of the original negative recommenda-tion. Their finding is normally made to an administrator who is probably the administrator immediately above the person against whom the grievance has been filed. (This is fortunate or unfortunate, depending upon your point of view.) That administrator must decide (of course, using the B.S. and L.I.E.) whether he will support the grievance committee, uphold the initial recommendation, or take any other action.

If the administrator who receives the grievance committee re-commendation wishes to support the grievance committee, it is usually a simple matter to justify this position. He merely states that the process of personal justice has worked; that the faculty member has had his day in court, and has presented sufficient evidence to merit the redress (remedy) that has been recommended, demonstrating the viability of the grievance machinery. An additional statement which might be made is that the recommendation of the grievance committee must, of necessity, be honored, or else there will be no need for such a committee. (As previously stated, "Necessity is the argument of those who have no good reason.") He feels compelled to accept their recommendation.

If, however, the administrator wishes to uphold the original negative recommendation and *not* accept the recommendation of the grievance committee, then he might reluctantly state that he does not wish to superimpose his judgment over that of the administrator who is closest to the situation. He reasons that this might undermine the authority of that person who, as a consequence, might therefore be viewed as powerless, and this might encourage more grievances for other negative recommendations (implying that this would be undesirable).

Of course the grievance committee might resign, or fail to accept other grievances if they feel that they have no power or that their recommendations hold no weight. These people are usually kept in line by accusations of being thin-skinned, quitters, cry-babies, etc.

Of course these same arguments can be used if the administrator reverses the original recommendation, and the administrator who made the initial recommendation threatens to quit. If that resignation is being sought, the other statements could be used and the grievance would probably be upheld despite the merits of the case.

Thus, Agile Administrators will continue making recommendations based upon the B.S. and L.I.E., remaining completely unconcerned about the grievance process and, as previously stated, in some cases secretly hoping that a grievance will materialize. The existence of a grievance committee is no constraining influence on the actions of Agile Administrators.

6.3   GETTING YOUR ADMINISTRATOR TO LIKE YOU

"The best way to get on in the world is to make people believe it's to their advantage to help you." – Jean de la Bruyere.

Throughout this book the point has been made that the only real criterion which will determine whether recommendations will be positive or negative is the personal likes or dislikes of the Agile Administrator. You should be convinced (unfortunately) that the Basic Supposition is used, the Law of Inverse Evaluation is in operation, and that Agile Administrators are an integral part of evaluation systems. The obvious question then becomes: "How can I get my Agile Administrator to like me, thus improving the chances that the B.S. and L.I.E. will operate in my favor instead of being used against me?"

I wish that it were not necessary for such a question to be asked, and that I were not compelled to comply. But since I have tried to point out some of the shortcomings of the faculty evaluation process, it seems that I would be only doing half a job if I did not give at least some advice on how to mitigate the adverse effects of the evils that have been identified.[6]

The question is difficult to answer because it is impossible for me to tell what would please the particular person who you wish to please . . . there are too many individual factors to classify conveniently.

At some institutions, there is a definite tendency to favor persons whose race, sex, religious affiliation, and ethnic background closely parallel those of the administration. Obviously, some of these factors are not easily changed. Either you have such characteristics or you don't! At some institutions those who maintain the status quo are rewarded; at others those who opt for progress and change get positive recommendations while the 'status quo-ers' are systematically weeded out of the system. The only way to improve your chances in the personnel evaluation lottery is to find out what your administrator likes. Try to appease him. (*"An appeaser is one who feeds a crocodile, hoping it will devour him last."* – Sir Winston Churchill.) Of course this may mean the loss of your self-esteem, but you must decide what price you are willing to pay for success. Apparently there is a sufficient number of people who are willing to pay almost any price to remain with their organizations.)

It really boils down to this: there are three ways that you can increase the chances that the B.S. and the L.I.E. will work in your favor.

1. You can get your administrator to *like* having you around.

---

[6]My reluctance to give advice can be summarized by this quote: "Only when a man is safely ensconced under six feet of earth, with several tons of enlauding granite upon his chest, is he in a position to give advice with any certainty, and then he is silent." Edward Newton.

There are several methods which may gain you the favor of your Agile Administrator.

2. You can get your administrator to *profit* from having your around.

3. You can *avoid* becoming someone he would rather not have around.

(1) Exhibit 22 summarizes the steps which one could take to try to gain a favorable impression with his Agile Administrator. These items cover a wide range of personal actions, but in summary they represent an honest (dishonest) effort to get along with the person who will be making personal assessments of your performance and qualifications. They are hints designed to get you to know that person, to get him to know you, and to try to understand behavior and actions which may on the surface appear to be arbitrary and capricious and which, in actuality, may be just that.

Of course, you run the risk that when you do those things which make your Agile Administrator like you, your peers will dislike you, either because they dislike the administrator and you are guilty by association, or because of the actions you take to get him to like you. (The L.I.E. again!) This is a calculated risk you must consider. But you can reduce this risk with a little forethought. What is the relative strength of the faculty against the administrator? Where is the power, and how can you align with that power? If the faculty has relatively little power in the faculty evaulation process, then you can probably afford to have them dislike you. If the faculty has the real power in such matters, then you would probably be wise to unite with the faculty against the common enemy. Maintaining alliances with the power group is just one of the power-acquisition strategies in organizations.[7]

There are side benefits which may lessen possible faculty hostility toward you. If you are able to get the Agile Administrator distracted from other matters, he may be too busy to take advantage of others, who may be thankful for your efforts (although they will not say so, nor will they reciprocate). You may even gain some informal influence over the Agile and use this to your advantage as well as to others, but this is fraught with dangers! A true Agile does not like to have anyone around who might erode his power or status. If you get any informal influence be sure to deny its existence, and do not, under any circumstances, give any impression that you have it, unless

---

[7]For a complete and thorough discussion of such techniques, see *Fundamentals of Organizational Behavior,* Andrew J. DuBrin, Pergammon Press, Inc., New York, 1974. Chapter 5, "Political Maneuvering in Organizations," suggests several methods, and includes additional career-advancement strategies (pp. 146–163).

EXHIBIT 22.
TECHNIQUES FOR GETTING YOUR ADMINISTRATOR TO LIKE YOU

1. Make your PEACE with him/her. ("You may win your peace, or buy it;—win it, by resistance to evil;—buy it, by compromise with evil." John Ruskin.)

2. Become a YES-MAN. ("Most people prefer a blunt 'Yes' to a polite and gracious 'No.' " Anon.)

3. Become an OPTIMIST. ("An optimist is one who makes the best of it when he gets the worst of it." Anon.)

4. Develop a FRIENDSHIP with him/her. ("A friendship is defined as a strong and habitual inclination between two persons to promote the good and happiness of one another." Eustace Budgell.)

5. Try to form an ALLIANCE with him/her. ("An alliance is a union of two thieves who have their hands so deeply inserted in each other's pockets that they cannot separately plunder a third." Ambrose Bierce.)

6. Make him/her HAPPY. ("Happiness is the perpetual possession of the well-decieved." Jonathan Swift.)

7. CHARM him/her. ("Charm is the ability to make someone feel that he is as wonderful as you are." Anon.)

8. FLATTER him/her. ("Flattery is simply telling the other person what he thinks of himself." Anon.)

9. Give him ADVICE. ("Advice is the suggestion you give someone else that you believe will work to your benefit." Anon.)

10. ADMIRE him. ("Admiration is polite recognition of another man's resemblance to ourselves." Ambrose Bierce.)

11. PRAISE him/her. ("Undeserved praise is satire in disguise." Anon.)

12. Become INTERESTED in him/her as a person. (We are interested in others when they are interested in us." Publicus Syrus.)

13. Be HUMBLE. ("Humility is a virtue all men preach, none practice, and everyone is content to hear." John Selden.)

14. Be MODEST. ("Modesty is the general art of enhancing your charm by pretending not to be aware of it." Oliver Herford.)

15. Don't be SELFISH. ("Selfishness is that detestible device which no one will forgive in others, and no one is without himself." Henry Ward Beecher.)

16. Be SELF-SACRIFICING. ("Self-sacrifice enables us to sacrifice others without blushing." George Bernard Shaw.)

17. Don't be PREJUDICED. ("Prejudice is an opinion which belongs to someone we dislike." Anon.)

18. Show your STYLE. ("Style is a wonderful pickle that is able to preserve mediocrity of thought under favorable conditions for many centuries." F. S. Oliver.)

19. Don't CRITICIZE him/her. ("Criticism is most effective when it sounds like praise." Arnold Glasow.)

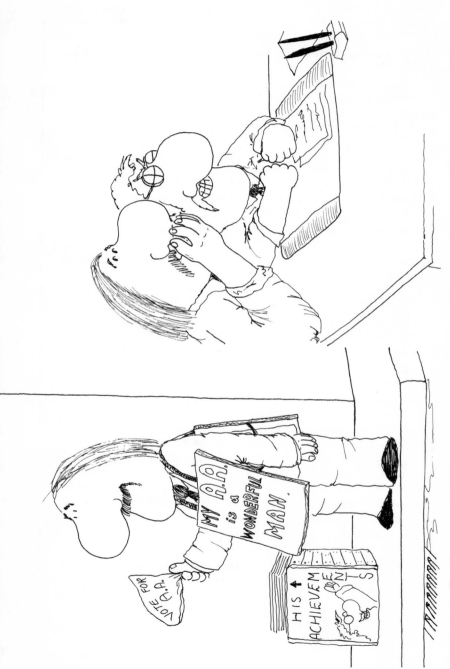

Touting your Administrator and keeping him "informed" may work wonders for you!

the Agile clearly views this as something that can be used to his personal benefit. It is a very tricky task to weave a fine line between having the Agile Administrator like you and having your peers like you at the same time. It can be done, but it won't be easy.

However, if you are able to get your Agile Administrator to like having you around, then you can be relatively certain that the Basic Supposition and the Law of Inverse Evaluation will be working more for than against you.

(2) You may also get the Agile Administrator to profit, financially and otherwise, by your presence. This can be done in several ways; only *four* will be suggested here.

    a) CONSULTING: You can become a "consulting contact" for him, finding consulting jobs for the administrator which (1) pay well, (2) require little preparation or work, and (3) may enhance his personal image of himself (if that is possible). After all, why shouldn't you share the wealth, since there is plenty of consulting to go around? Properly handled, this will cost you nothing out of your own pocket, but may pay rich dividends in terms of personnel actions.

    b) PUBLISHING: You can become his "publication partner," securing publications for the Agile which may enhance his personal reputation (at least in his eyes, if not in anyone else's). You could do this by having friends of yours who are on Editorial Review Boards of journals do you a small favor. You might volunteer to co-author a publication with him, *after* you have it virtually completed. This kills several birds with one stone. You and he both get a publication which is scholarly and a contribution. How could it be otherwise with *his name* on it? This gives you a positive piece of data in the research/publications criterion. It costs you nothing except the loss of an individual publication. (At some institutions co-authored publications have more status than individually prepared ones. They just seem more scholarly!) You may, if you are publishing some of your own work, drop in a quote or two from some of his published material, assuming that any exists. In short, you can help establish and broaden your Agile Administrator's publication reputation while solidifying your own. This 'flunky role' won't appeal to some, but if you want to know how to get your Agile Administrator to like you, this is one way that has worked for others.

c) PUBLIC RELATIONS: You may become your Agile Administrator's unpaid and unheralded public relations agent, securing speaking engagements for him and finding other community interest activities that appeal to him. Some of these might be uncovered as a result of your activities in the local (and broader) community. Others could be the direct result of a conscious effort to find them for the administrator. Ideal speeches are ones which require no preparation, insure a large audience (captive ones), and which pay large honorariums, in cash. In this way you are helping to enhance and broaden the image of the Agile. For this he must certainly consider you someone personally desirable to have around.

d) HIS PROMOTION/ADVANCEMENT: If your Agile Administrator has loftier ambitions, you can capitalize on them by helping him achieve these aims. Your efforts in Consulting, Public Relations, and Research/Publications will help, but you could also give him pieces of information which might be useful in advancing his own career. (You might reread the material in DuBrin's book referred to in footnote 7, and adapt it to this purpose.) Carried to an extreme, this role of information provider can deteriorate into an informant's role. You should be aware of this possibility and draw the line where your conscience dictates. (*"Conscience is the sixth sense that comes to our aid when we are doing wrong and tells us that we are about to get caught."* – Anon.)[8]

One additional word of caution is in order. If your Agile has reached his "level of incompetence" and does not wish to advance further in the administrative hierarchy, then you must not support or encourage any efforts that might threaten him with a promotion. Preparing a person who doesn't want to be advanced, for an advancement can be very threatening, and he may view you as someone who is helping him *out* (out of the organization), and therefore place you as a prime candidate for the "must-go" list.

(3) The third way that you might be able to get your Agile Administrator to like you is to avoid becoming someone whom he dis-

---

[8]"What is moral is what you feel good after, and what is immoral is what you feel bad after, assuming one has a conscience." Adapted from Ernest Hemingway.

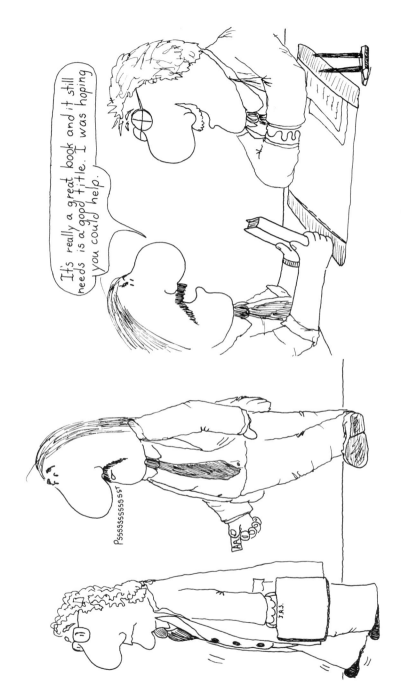

Providing Public Relations assistance and "co-authoring" with your Administrator may swing the Basic Supposition and Law of Inverse Evaluation into your favor!

likes having around—people on his "to-go" or "to-get" list. Becoming someone whom he likes to have around and making it profitable for him to keep you around are certainly two steps in that direction, but there are other measures that can be taken to solidify your position within the organization. You must find out what kind of an organization he wants, what amount and kind of progress, change, or status quo he desires, and contribute towards achieving these objectives.

You must avoid becoming a threat to the Agile Administrator. This may happen if you are liked too much by peers and/or subordinates and thereby take some of the glory away from your Agile. You must cooperate, not compete, with him. You must avoid becoming too successful (either in teaching, consulting, research, etc.) without either sharing your success with him (if he will accept a share) or keeping your success a secret. Agile Administrators don't particularly like having bright and shining stars around them; it makes the administrator's shine that much less brilliant.[9] If you are successful at consulting (that is, you make a lot of money) then you must deny it at every opportunity and continue to plead poverty at every moment. You might even apologize for your apparent success. (*"To apologize is to lay the foundation for a future offense."* – Ambrose Bierce.) That is, unless the Agile Administrator likes having successes around and is also successful. (You should tell him that he is successful regardless of the actual situation.) And if he claims the credit for your success, give him credit! In summary, you must avoid becoming a threat, a disruptive force, a competitor, a thorn in the side of your Agile Administrator. Thorns are easily removed, and seldom left in place. But if you are successful at getting your Agile Administrator to like having you around, then the B.S. and L.I.E. just might work in your favor. (*"Success is often hard to take especially when it's the other fellow's."* – Anon.)

6.4   IMPLICATIONS

"The personnel evaluation process is a perpetual caricature of itself; and every moment it is the mockery and the contradiction of what it is pretending to be." – Adapted from George Santayana.

What are the implications of Agile Administrators, using the Basic Supposition and the Law of Inverse Evaluation?

---

[9]"Success makes us intolerant of failure, and failure makes us intolerant of success." William Feather.

The Agile Administrator: As long as there are Agile Administrators in the personnel evaluation process, there will not be an evaluation system, only a justification system. Competence will continue to be redefined as the ability to cater to the personal whims of the A.A., and those who wish to share in the rewards of the system will have to accept this concept of competence.

The Basic Supposition: No matter what criteria are published and are stated as those upon which performance and qualification will be judged, only one criterion will, in fact, be used: the personal likes and dislikes of the Agile Administrator. Those whom he likes will get positive recommendations, and those not in his favor will receive negative recommendations. Data is meaningless. The message is clear. Concentrate your efforts towards developing a harmonious relationship with your Agile Administrator. This won't eliminate the B.S., but it may give it a little nudge in your direction and have it working in your favor, not against you.

The Law of Inverse Evaluation: Since this is a law of human behavior, it must be obeyed until it is repealed. Don't spend time wishing that it did not exist! It does! Instead, put all your energies into getting on the right side of the law. You can do this by the judicious presentation and interpretation of data, selecting the right data to submit for evaluation or ignore, and in general getting the Basic Supposition working for you.

The next time you see a recommendation which appears to be at polar extremes with the data used to support it, look very carefully. You may be witnessing, firsthand, an Agile Administrator operating under the Basic Supposition and using the Law of Inverse Evaluation.

Bibliography

Armour, Richard, *Going Around in Academic Circles,* McGraw-Hill Book Company, N.Y., N.Y., 1965.

DuBrin, Andrew J., *Fundamentals of Organizational Behavior,* Pergammon Press, N.Y., N.Y., 1974.

Galbraith, John Kenneth, *Economics and the Public Purpose,* Houghton Mifflin Company, Boston, Mass., 1973.

Herzog, Arthur, *The B.S. Factor,* Simon and Schuster, N.Y., N.Y., 1973.

Huff, Darrell, *How to Lie with Statistics,* W. W. Norton and Co., Inc., N.Y., N.Y., 1954.

Peter, Lawrence J., *The Peter Prescription,* William Marrow and Company, Inc., N.Y., N.Y., 1972.

Porter, Lee, *Degrees for Sale,* Arco Publishing Co., Inc., N.Y., N.Y., 1972.

Van Den Berghe, Peter, *Academic Gamesmanship,* Abelard-Schuman, London, England, 1970.